BRIGHT NOTES

THE OCTOPUS BY FRANK NORRIS

Intelligent Education

Nashville, Tennessee

BRIGHT NOTES: The Octopus
www.BrightNotes.com

No part of this publication may be used or reproduced in any manner whatsoever without written permission, except in the case of brief quotations in critical articles and reviews. For permissions, contact Influence Publishers http://www.influencepublishers.com.

ISBN: 978-1-645421-30-6 (Paperback)
ISBN: 978-1-645421-31-3 (eBook)

Published in accordance with the U.S. Copyright Office Orphan Works and Mass Digitization report of the register of copyrights, June 2015.

Originally published by Monarch Press.
Eric J. Solibakke, 1966
2019 Edition published by Influence Publishers.

Interior design by Lapiz Digital Services. Cover Design by Thinkpen Designs.

Printed in the United States of America.

Library of Congress Cataloging-in-Publication Data forthcoming.
Names: Intelligent Education
Title: BRIGHT NOTES: The Octopus
Subject: STU004000 STUDY AIDS / Book Notes

CONTENTS

1) Introduction to Frank Norris   1

2) An Essay On Norris's Style to The Octopus   9

3) Textual Analysis
    Book I: Chapter One   15
    Book I: Chapter Two   20
    Book I: Chapter Three   25
    Book I: Chapter Four   29
    Book I: Chapter Five   33
    Book I: Chapter Six   38
    Book II: Chapter One   43
    Book II: Chapter Two   47
    Book II: Chapter Three   51
    Book II: Chapter Four   55
    Book II: Chapter Five   59
    Book II: Chapter Six   62
    Book II: Chapter Seven   66
    Book II: Chapter Eight   71
    Book II: Chapter Nine   76
    Book II: Chapter Ten   81

4)	Character Analyses	83
5)	Critical Commentary	95
6)	Essay Questions and Answers	98
7)	Bibliography	102

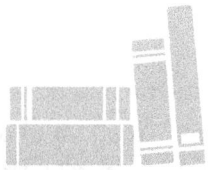

INTRODUCTION TO FRANK NORRIS

EARLY LIFE

Frank Norris was born in March, 1870, in Chicago. His father was a businessman who provided well for the family and his mother was an actress who retired from the stage when she married. His mother kept alive her dramatic interests by reading to the family from Scott, Dickens, and Stevenson.

As an eight-year-old boy, Norris made his first trip to Europe. When he was fourteen years old the family moved to San Francisco. As he grew older, Norris was expected to follow in the footsteps of his father in business. He was sent to business school where he suffered miserably from lack of interest. He showed some talent at drafting, and finally convinced his family to allow him to attend art school in San Francisco, where he progressed fairly well although he did not evidence great talent.

MIDDLE LIFE

In 1877 his family took him to Paris to study art, as was the custom at that time. He enrolled at the Bouguereau Studio and did rather poorly as an art student. He adventured around Paris with many bohemian characters of the type who converged on the city to study art. He had no responsibilities and no economic problems, giving him great freedom to develop his imagination and exercise his taste for adventure in the exciting surroundings of Paris.

Norris's father returned to San Francisco soon after the family arrived. Before the year was out, his mother and younger brother, Charles, also returned to San Francisco, leaving the seventeen-year-old Norris in Paris alone to carry on his studies. Led perhaps by a love of romantic literature instilled by his mother, Norris developed a profound interest in medieval literature, notably Froissart's *Chronicles*, and in the trappings of the medieval era, armor, costumes, and weapons. His time and effort were divided between adventures with his friends in the city, medieval studies, and a game of lead soldiers, which he had begun with his younger brother before Charles had returned to San Francisco. They invented a war with the soldiers, and Norris became so involved with the medieval game that he named many of the characters and filled in their histories in detail. After Charles left Paris, the game continued by mail. Norris spent little time at the studio, and more time writing. The letters to his brother became very elaborate and he wrote an article on medieval armor which he sent to his mother. It appeared in the *San Francisco Chronicle* in March 1889.

His father realized that Norris's art studies were not advancing and ordered the boy back to San Francisco. He arrived in New York with sideburns, spats, walking stick, and all the regalia of a Paris dandy and a trunk full of medieval mementos. In San Francisco he seemed to be at loose ends, having abandoned his war game with Charles. His passion for medieval romance took form in a three-canto narrative poem, *Yvernelle*.

He attended the University of California at Berkeley for four years, more a social than a scholarly occupation. Having refused to learn algebra, he never received a diploma from the university. He grew tired of medievalism and his interest turned toward contemporary literature. Kipling was his first modern love, and the discovery of Zola followed soon after. He developed a passion for the French naturalist, whom he called a romantic because he selected extraordinary characters and threw them into a terrible environment, full of monstrous powers and influences, with a vague note of terror quivering in the background. He considered naturalism a form of romanticism, a fundamental misunderstanding which he never clarified. He was never able to accept all of the tenets of naturalism, notably its faith in science and the scientific method, and its ultimate acceptance of determinism over free will.

When he left Berkeley, Norris's family separated, depriving him of his right to his father's money. He was sobered by the realization that he would have to support himself. In 1894 he went to Harvard to study writing seriously. With few friends and a dislike of the conservative, intellectual atmosphere of the eastern university, Norris found much time to concentrate on writing. He wrote the bulk of two novels simultaneously, *Vandover and the Brute*, and *McTeague*.

ADULT LIFE

When he left Harvard, convinced that an hour of experience is worth more than ten years of study, he went to Africa to gain experience. By chance he arrived in Johannesburg just before the Jameson Raid. It was a bloodless revolution, but Norris filled his letters with interesting observations, resulting in a contract with the San Francisco Chronicle to be its correspondent.

Suddenly he came down with malaria, and returned to San Francisco to convalesce.

He took a position on the Wave in San Francisco and wrote editorials, reviews, features, sports, and short fiction for it, acquiring a large and useful experience. He took time off to complete *McTeague* for publication. *Moran of the Lady Letty*, a short adventure novel based on stories related to him by a local sea captain, appeared in installments in the Wave. As a result of *Moran of the Lady Letty*, Norris secured a position in New York, working for S. S. McClure.

In New York he had little income and lived in rather uncomfortable circumstances. He met W. D. Howells, the dean of American critics, who praised *McTeague*, which he read in manuscript.

With the coming of the Spanish American War in Cuba, Norris was sent down to the island as a correspondent, not without a great deal of enthusiasm on his part. After several months in Cuba, Norris was stricken with a recurrence of malaria that sent him to San Francisco to recover his strength. While there he received the first copies of *Moran of the Lady Letty*, published by Doubleday, McClure, and Company, his first published novel. He set out writing *A Man's Woman*, also based on the stories told by his sea captain friend. Much of the horror he experienced in Cuba found its way into this book, and he considered it his worst. In February, 1899, *McTeague* came out, and another novel, *Blix*, was accepted for publication. *McTeague* caused a small tempest, and most reviewers damned the book as immoral and brutal. Howells praised it in his column, and Norris was, in general, pleased with the book's reception, although it sold poorly.

At this point, Norris conceived the idea for a series of novels "as big as all outdoors." The first was to be a story of California, which produces wheat, the second a story of Chicago, which distributes it, and the third a story of Europe, which consumes the wheat to avert a famine. Once he had decided on the general direction of his **epic** trilogy, he began to collect information and incidents. He returned to California to observe and collect data first hand. After selecting the Mussel Slough Affair, an event in the expansion of the Southern Pacific Railroad where seven men were killed over land rights, he researched in newspapers and through interviews until he felt competent to handle the incident as the **climax** of the first novel in the trilogy. He discovered other characters, like Charles Evans, a train robber, who was metamorphosed into Dyke in *The Octopus*. He rearranged the geography of California by transferring Tulare to the flat wheat lands in the San Joaquin Valley and calling the town Bonneville. A barn dance and a rabbit hunt occurred while he was there and found their way into two chapters of the book.

After four months of research and note-taking, he returned to New York, where he interviewed Collis P. Huntington, the railroad magnate, to hear the railroad's side of the controversy. He worked methodically for a year on *The Octopus*, organizing, summarizing, tabulating, arranging his notes, and creating each of the characters in outline. The great danger, he felt, was to degenerate to propaganda for social change. He wanted to present the truth without bias. It was the drama of the Mussel Slough Affair, the clash between producer and distributor, which attracted him, not its social implications.

Some of the characters he wanted to live, others he wanted to be types, and still others to be symbols. He felt that he must have enough characters to give a cross-section of California in the 1880s, and that their social classes and environments must be shown, along with their motives. The characteristics of many of the characters were drawn from his friends and acquaintances. For example, Mrs. Cedarquist is drawn from the chairman of a woman's literary society, to whom Norris's mother introduced him in San Francisco. Angele Varian and her daughter Angele were to be symbolic characters, opposed to Hilma Tree, as moonlight to sunlight, the one mysterious and ephemeral, the other hale and strong.

During the same year, Norris became a reader for Doubleday, Page and Company, which gave him enough income to marry. That summer he read the manuscript of Theodore Dreiser's *Sister Carrie* for his company and began a campaign to get it published. His social life became a burden, and he moved to Roselle, New Jersey, for solitude. On December 15, 1900, he delivered the manuscript of *The Octopus* to his publisher. Immediately on publication of the novel, Norris became famous. For the second volume of the trilogy, Norris moved to Chicago, where he began a study of markets and distribution in much the same way he had researched *The Octopus*. He found the research difficult and returned to New York without a clear understanding of the business processes. Money was still scarce and he resumed short story writing to pay for his daughter who was born in February, 1902. He also wrote the hasty essays which are collected under the title, *The Responsibilities of a Novelist*, containing his declaration of faith in literature. After many false starts and painful revisions, he finished *The Pit*, second novel of the trilogy, and returned to California.

For the third novel, *The Wolf*, he planned to sail slowly around the world, observing the consumption of wheat, and selecting a small country in which to set the action. Just before they were to leave, his wife came down with appendicitis and submitted to surgery successfully. A month later, Norris felt it.

Although his wife and friends feared appendicitis, he refused to go to the hospital. He appeared to improve, but a few days later he was wracked with agony. The doctor operated and found advanced peritonitis, which his body, weakened by malaria, was unable to throw off. He died October 25, 1902, at the age of thirty-two, and was buried in Oakland, California.

NORRIS AND NATURALISM - REALISM - ROMANTICISM

Norris's understanding of naturalism was faulty and he could never overcome an innate romanticism. In general, naturalism is a school of literature which developed in France with the works of Flaubert, Zola, and others. Zola made the most consistent statement of the objectives of the school in *The Experimental Novel*. The three basic issues of naturalism are determinism, the influence of environment, and the objective literary style. According to naturalism, all life is governed by impersonal laws, which can be discovered, analyzed, and used in a novel, much the way the laws of physics can be used to repeat experiments, with similar results each time. The great study of naturalists is the environment of man, its influence on the man and his on it. The social milieu is of prime importance, and through close observation of the social milieu and the man, the laws of determinism can be discovered and their effects traced. In the matter of style, naturalism dictates rigid objectivity. Rhetoric has no place. The opinions of the author are superfluous. Only the show of events is important, never the philosophical why. Lyricism is chaotic and untruthful, according to Zola, and a great style is composed of logic and clarity.

In theory, the subjects taken by a naturalist and a realist for a novel are not important, and the literary techniques are very similar. The line of demarcation between the two schools is vague and difficult to trace. In both schools the novelist must not avoid material merely because it is unpleasant to read or to contemplate. Misery and sordidness have their place in life, perhaps even the dominant place. The fundamental difference between the two schools is the philosophic assumption of determinism that underlies naturalism. Determinism removes the element of free will from human conduct and leads to a pessimistic point of view. **Realism** is a nonphilosophical style that arrives at no conclusion.

Romanticism is opposed to both naturalism and **realism** by its emphasis on the exotic and unusual, and by its emotional approach toward life. The heightening of emotion found in romanticism is achieved through a literary style which communicates the emotional attitude of the author. The style is consequently opposed to the logic and clarity sought by naturalist and realist alike.

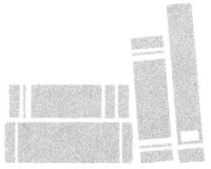

THE OCTOPUS

AN ESSAY ON NORRIS'S STYLE

....

DIRECTNESS AND RHETORIC

In his essays on the craft of novel writing, Norris recommends a prose style of simplicity and directness. In *The Octopus*, he writes a number of passages in a simple and direct style, but very often he slips into a rhapsodic style of rhetorical and "poetic" triteness. His prose style in general suffers from a lack of economy, produced both by his choice of vocabulary and by his typical sentence structure. Very often a simple declarative sentence is weighed down by a string of adjectives, qualifying phrases, oppositions, and modifying clauses. The effect is a piling up of meaning like the building up of earth in front of a bulldozer blade, and the precision of the sentence is sacrificed. Although he is not a consistent originator of striking and clever figures of speech, his prose is occasionally brightened by an especially apt and original figure. He has a tendency to personify massive and powerful forces - and he dearly loves grandeur, like Wheat, Life, People, and so on.

When Norris describes the Wheat, imbuing it with a natural force of its own, he commits the greatest travesty of language.

The rhetorical loftiness of those passages is intended to project the grandeur of the natural force, but in general has the reverse effect by tainting the Wheat with a cast of ridiculousness. The over-all accomplishment is trite and repetitious. Norris does not attempt to avoid repetition. Before writing the novel he wrote sketches of the major characters and gave them epithets and mannerisms which he repeats nearly every time the character appears. The purpose of those repetitions is to approach the **epic** style of Homer, whose characters are always identifiable by a stock epithet. A good example is Osterman's slit-like mouth.

DIALOGUE

In *The Octopus*, the dialogue tends to be carefully matched to the character of the speaker and to have a ring of authenticity. Magnus Derrick, for example, usually speaks with the slightly affected tone of end-of-the-century political oratory. Norris avoids differences of dialect in this novel, with the exception of Hooven, to whom Norris gives a thick accent leaded with Germanisms.

REPETITION

In general, Norris's style bears the imprint of carelessness and haste, which accurately reflects his temperament and the manner in which he worked. He is repetitious and "redolent" with clichés. He drives home an impression, a manner, an observation, a characteristic, a **theme** with hammer blows. At its best, his style is dramatic and spare. The gunfight between the League and the railroad men at the irrigation ditch is an example of his best naturalistic prose style.

LIMITATIONS OF THE EPIC APPROACH

Norris and several American journalists who reviewed *The Octopus* when it was first published spoke of the novel as an American **epic**. The primary qualities they based their judgments on are the novel's historical content, the elevated style of much of its prose, and its grandiose scope of characters and setting. The novel is without a doubt an extremely fictionalized account of an actual event in the history of California, and it also reflects the attitude of large business enterprises during the period at the end of the nineteenth century. An elevated prose style is associated with **epics** through the work of Milton and the commonly read English translations of Homer and Virgil. Responsible critics have been forced to admit that Norris's elevated prose style is more trite than meaningful, making the book less **epic** than it would have been had he not strained so hard to approximate an **epic** style. Although an **epic** usually has a **protagonist**, which *The Octopus* does not have, an **epic** also has a vast number of characters and a large theater of action. *The Octopus* approaches closest to an **epic** in this respect than in any other. Norris inhabits this novel with both country and city people of several social classes. Some of those characters are closely observed and accurately located in their environments. Others are stiff and unconvincing to the reader, because they are mere types rather than living characters.

JUXTAPOSITION OF PERSPECTIVES

Norris's point of view as author of *The Octopus* is olympian. He does not make all of the action occur to a **protagonist** or observer, nor does the reader see all of the action through the eyes or mind of one man. Often Norris writes directly to the reader, removing the reader from the dramatic circumstances of the book while he listens to the author's voice. When Norris describes the wheat "wrapped in Nirvanic calm," he is speaking in his own voice. At other times the dramatic action is seen through Presley's mind, as if Presley and the author were the same man. The dramatic action is handled that way, for example, in Chapter One and in the scene of Presley's last visit to the San Joaquin Valley, where he observes the conditions of his few remaining friends. The author's voice occasionally speaks directly through Presley's lips. The best example of it occurs during Presley's last visit to the Valley when he suddenly decides that the world is made up of invincible "forces." At other times the reader feels the author's presence by the mobility of the point of view. Two grand scenes are written in that style - the barn dance and the jackrabbit hunt. In both scenes, the author moves quickly and effectively from close observation of individuals to sweeping generalizations and descriptions of the over-all dramatic action.

STRUCTURE

The novel has a simple basic structure of direct narrative, except for its several faults. It covers approximately one year, or one growing cycle of the wheat, without flashbacks or awkward passages of parallel time. Complications in the structure are introduced by the story of Vanamee, which goes along simultaneously and seldom touches the events that occupy the other characters. His story is rather episodic and inessential except as Vanamee advises Presley or helps him to important conclusions that affect his conduct. The most serious defect in the structure is the chapter devoted to the fates of Mrs. Hooven and Minna. It is uncalled for by the events of the book, but tends to support Norris's **themes** by showing again the consequences of social injustice. In addition, those scenes allow Norris to elaborate his handling of the city, a necessary inclusion for the **epic** purpose of enlarging the reader's acquaintance with the setting of the novel.

THEMATIC DEVELOPMENT

The major **theme** supported by the dramatic action of the novel is that the corruptive influence of business, as an expression of man's desire for wealth and power, is stronger than the ability of uncorrupted men to resist it. Good men are driven to destruction by the P. and S. W., first by causing them to corrupt their goodness by adapting unethical modes of conduct, and then by killing them if they remain in the railroad's path of expansion. Along with that **theme**, however, runs the idea that the affairs of men are the result of universal forces that control the universe from afar without regard for man. The activities of men are chance actions outside of the great movements of the universe. A second major **theme** supported by the dramatic action is that love will cause the desirable elements of a man's character to assume precedence over undesirable elements. The conclusion of the novel is not a theme supported by the dramatic action. It is, however, a **theme** to the extent that a character in the novel formulates the idea based on his knowledge of the events described in the dramatic action. The idea is that all things are good if viewed from sufficient perspective. The four major **themes** or ideas supported by the book or advanced by its author are, according to most responsible critics, irreconcilable. Their conclusion is that the book is flawed from the point of view of its development of themes.

THE OCTOPUS AS NATURALISM

The technique of naturalistic writing produces an objective, journalistic style, with little indication of the author's presence. A good example of Norris's naturalistic style is the story of the capture of Dyke by the posse. The **episode** begins in Chapter Five, when Dyke shows up on the Quien Sabe Ranch to get a fresh horse from Annixter. From that point on, the narrative is very objective and detailed, without an emotional cast lent to it by the author. Of course, the reader has an emotional attitude toward Dyke, but it is established in the preceding pages.

Other parts that are written in the naturalistic style are the skirmish at the irrigation ditch and the stories of Minna Hooven and her mother. In the later story, the author complicates his presentation of the facts by mixing it between paragraphs describing the dinner at the Gerards. The dinner is satirical, rather than naturalistic, and the over-all accomplishment of the chapter is ironical. **Irony** properly belongs to the naturalistic style, because it is produced by the author's juxtaposition of events so that the reader has more knowledge of what is happening than the characters to whom it is happening. **Satire** has little place in naturalism since satire is a way of writing in which the author belittles his characters and their actions by communicating an attitude that will permit the reader to judge the characters and actions in a certain way, usually ridiculous. It is a violation of objectivity.

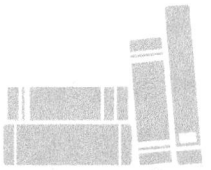

THE OCTOPUS

TEXTUAL ANALYSIS

BOOK I: CHAPTER ONE

Initial impressions of California's San Joaquin Valley are given through the eyes of Presley, the main character in the novel, as he makes a long trip through the geographical area where the bulk of the story will take place. Presley meets Hooven, an immigrant farmer living on the Los Muertos Ranch, who asks Presley to intercede for him to ensure that he not be discharged from the ranch for reason of economy. Harran Derrick, son of the owner of Los Muertos, whom Presley next visits, introduces the central conflict of the book, the fight between the farmers and the Pacific and Southwestern Railroad. Continuing his trip, Presley encounters Dyke, a railroad engineer who is to be unfairly discharged from his job on the railroad. At Guadalajara, Presley listens to an old Mexican tell stories of the early, romantic days of California. Presley stops at the Quien Sabe Ranch to visit his friend Annixter, owner of the ranch. Later Presley meets Vanamee, who, as a result of the loss of the woman he loved, has become a mystical, hermitic figure in the Valley. Presley leaves Vanamee at the Mission of San Juan and continues to his favorite hideaway in the foothills. The land of California grows to romantically **epic** proportions in Presley's poetic imagination. The epic tone is suddenly destroyed by a train that slaughters several sheep on the tracks and nearly runs down Presley.

COMMENT

The Octopus begins with a sweeping description of a land which builds to **epic** proportions by the end of the chapter, only to be suddenly reduced to the ugly and commonplace by the intrusion and power of the railroad. The force of the land, which Norris often describes as the mystical force of nature, and the force of the railroad, which he describes as a powerful force of evil and oppression, created by man, are the two forces which Norris will present as locked in deadly conflict throughout the book. A **theme** of *The Octopus* is the ability of a giant corporation created by men to corrupt and destroy human beings who oppose it.

The first person whom Presley meets, Hooven, a common farmer, a little man, is in danger of losing his livelihood as an indirect result of the railroad. The owner of Los Muertos, Magnus Derrick, may have to discharge him for economic reasons. There is a great deal of fear in his voice when he asks Presley to intercede on his behalf. Harran Derrick also talks about the progress of the railroad against the interests of the farmers. The crop has been unsuccessful because of a lack of rain. The price of grain shipment to tidewater remains high, cutting deeply into the ranchers' profits. They have lodged a case against the railroad. Harran announces to Presley the loss of the case in court. The reader is prepared by Harran's remarks and the tone of foreboding in his voice for a continuation of the fight to a climax.

The story told by Dyke, whom Presley runs into after he leaves Harran, continues the story of the unfair, almost irrational conduct of the railroad. Dyke has been a loyal employee, but he is discharged without regard for his need to support his family or his loyalty to the railroad. Dyke's story alerts the reader to the nature of the power of the railroad over human beings who come in contact with it.

Another fundamental **theme** in *The Octopus*, a philosophical theme which engaged Norris during his adult life, is set out through Presley's eyes as a basic conflict between romantic old California and realistic new California. The old Mexican in Guadalajara, whom Presley listens to raptly, tells romantic stories of the old California. Presley is interested in the new California, but he cannot reconcile himself to it. To him the new California seems sordid and petty compared to the high style and chivalry of the old country before the coming of economic power and the railroad.

The new California is a matter of business, power, money, and profit. Notice that Presley did not seem moved by Harran's announcement that the farmers had lost their case in court. He is profoundly moved, however, by the story the old Mexican tells.

The **themes** of the book will be reflected in the changes in Presley's personality as he comes to realize the immediacy and depth of the power struggle between the farmers and the railroad. As the reader will see, the **themes** of the book are shown in the changes which come over four men: Presley, Magnus Derrick, Annixter, and Vanamee. All four are permanently and profoundly changed by the struggle.

Annixter is introduced as a rather bitter man, out of sorts with himself and his surroundings. He is plagued by problems he does not understand. He is uncomfortable. Although intelligent, he lacks insights about himself. The relationship between Presley and Annixter must be noted very carefully. They have a kind of masculine love for each other that is extremely important to Annixter. At the beginning of the book, Presley is Annixter's only friend, the only person he responds to positively.

The story of Vanamee's love for Angele, her violent death, and the long period of wandering and asceticism that follows illustrates Norris's point of view that the universe is full of irrational forces that shape human conduct. The man who destroyed Angele is never found, as if he were a kind of enigma who came to destroy the love between the two young people because they were too happy. Vanamee's conduct cannot be understood with the rational mind. He is a man close to nature whose character is instinctive. As Norris says, Vanamee is a natural poet, as opposed to Presley, who is a rational or willful poet. Presley's character is sufficiently broad that, while being a friend of that most unpoetic Annixter, he can also be a friend of Vanamee, the instinctive mythmaker and poet.

Presley's obsession to write the great **epic** poem of the West is illustrated by his mistaken belief that the **epic** period is past. When Presley reads a section from the Odyssey while alone in the foothills and under the influence of his imagination, the California landscape grows to enormous proportions. The tone of Norris's writing changes when he describes the land. He evokes the size, the force, the fertility, and the permanence of the land while belittling the works of man on the face of it. The land inspires Presley's imagination to grasp the outlines of his great **epic**. However, Presley's **epic** vision must ignore the truth about the struggle over the land for wealth and power. To the extent that he ignores that struggle, his epic is false.

While he is still under the influence of the "force of nature," as the land can honestly be called, the speeding locomotive slams through the herd of sheep, scattering carcasses along the tracks. Presley himself is nearly killed. The train smacks into his consciousness like some unnamable force of powerful evil that perverts the beauty and naturalness of the land. The passage of the locomotive destroys his **epic** vision and leaves Presley shaken.

The structure of this opening chapter is very simple. It is a business chapter, where several of the main characters and main **themes** and the author's point of view are introduced with little or no progress in the plot. There is no single person through whom the events of the struggle between the farmers and the railroad are viewed. Often it appears that Norris identifies with Presley. But not always. Norris maintains an author's point of view, which allows him to switch from scene to scene and from character to character with great freedom. The opening chapter reads very much like a description by film, with the eye of the camera surveying the length and breadth of the land, stopping to introduce characters it meets while moving through the valley.

THE OCTOPUS

TEXTUAL ANALYSIS

BOOK I: CHAPTER TWO

....

Harran Derrick goes through the morning chores on the Los Muertos Ranch, and then leaves for Bonneville to meet his father, Magnus, who is returning on the train from the unsuccessful court fight in San Francisco. Magnus and Harran meet S. Behrman, the local railroad spokesman, at the train station and they argue about the railroad. On their way back to the ranch, the two men stop off at the Quien Sabe Ranch to invite Annixter for dinner and a ranchers' meeting. S. Behrman arrives to protest the killing of the sheep, putting the blame on Annixter for having a faulty fence. Magnus, Harran, and Behrman leave, and the scene shifts to Annixter and his fascination with Hilma Tree. Annixter, angered by reasons he cannot understand, leaves for Los Muertos Ranch in a downpour of rain. He meets Delany on the road and fires him after a short argument.

COMMENT

The long description of Harran Derrick's morning on the Los Muertos Ranch helps the reader to understand how profoundly important the land is to a rancher, and how all the events of his life are influenced by his land. The description contains what is often called "local color," which is necessary to the literary technique of naturalism. The short scene where Harran examines the wheat and discusses the process of bluestoning is not essential to plot or character development in the novel. It is the kind of information which gives verisimilitude to the book and the sense that the events in it, although universal in their implications about human nature, took place at a specific location on the face of the earth, California.

A paragraph buried in the story of Harran's morning chores acquaints the reader further with the extent of the ranchers' economic problems. The price of wheat has steadily declined as the structure of distribution has grown larger and more powerful. Instead of merely the wheat grower having to make his living from the grain, all the middlemen also have to make their fortunes, "the commission merchant, the elevator combine, the mixing-house ring, the banks, the warehousemen, the laboring man, and above all, the railroad." In addition, the crop has been poor for two years as a result of lack of rain. Harran is depressed and gloomy when he visualizes the extent of the ranchers' problems. When he realizes that the following year will probably be an excellent growing year, his mood grows foreboding because a good crop means a lot of money. A lot of money means that the railroad fight will become more acute.

Norris, as author, is emotionally on the side of the wheat growers. By his careful, sympathetic introductions of them, and his detailed **exposition** of their problems, he aligns the reader's sympathies with them also. All of the ranchers are likable characters, and basically "good" men.

Mrs. Derrick, Harran's mother, is presented as an attractive woman, although a little shallow and foolish, and very much out of touch with the magnitude of the struggle facing her husband and all the ranchers. Norris wants the reader to realize that the farmers are only human beings, intelligent and aware, who are caught in a trap of oppression. It would defeat his purpose in the novel if the reader were to consider a farmer some kind of subhuman beast of burden who toiled day in and day out like a trained animal, to bring food to the tables of civilized people.

Magnus Derrick, whom Harran meets at the railroad station in Bonneville that morning, is an imposing character, whose fall in the course of the book has the proportions of tragedy. When Magnus describes the farmers' failure in court, the reader can feel the trap tighten around the farmers. They fight the power of the railroad with all of the moral and legal force they have, but they are losing the fight. They will have to take up different kinds of weapons.

S. Behrman, the local railroad representative, arrives at the station and the three men fall into an argument about the unfair practices of the railroad. Magnus's plows are sitting there in the station but he cannot have them because they must first be checked through the railroad company shipping depot in San Francisco. The railroad is an enormous bureaucracy, even in those early days, and their regulations must be slavishly followed without regard to the actual needs of their clients. Magnus needs the plows at a certain time, dependent on the progression of the seasons, a factor he cannot control. The railroad, by contract, needs to send the plows to San Francisco before Magnus can have them only because someone has arbitrarily organized the shipment of goods in that fashion. Behrman, who could scarcely be presented as a more reptilian man, argues with Magnus in the classical manner of a bureaucrat. He continually defers to higher authority and claims total lack of responsibility on his part. He is only doing his job as he has been ordered to do it. He knows nothing. He is responsible for nothing. He is a representative without authority to change the conduct of the company, even in so small a matter as unloading the plows. Not only are Harran and Magnus unsatisfied in the argument, but their dignity is attacked by having to present serious suit and abide by the decision of a man whom they cannot in any way respect. Behrman is the new kind of man, brought into the valley by the coming business power, who has no morality beyond opportunism and loyalty to his central office.

While the Derrick men are at Annixter's, where they have stopped off on their way back to Los Muertos to invite Annixter to the ranch for dinner and a ranchers' meeting, Behrman arrives and accuses Annixter of negligence. It was a hole in Annixter's fence that allowed the sheep to be on the railroad in front of the locomotive. Behrman's manner is so offensive that no man could honorably accept his allegations, and of course the reader has already seen that Annixter is not the kind of man of admit guilt. The issue is equivocal, because it is true that the hole in Annixter's fence did allow the sheep to be on the track. However, because they were, there is no reason to slaughter them. If the sheep had escaped onto the land of another farmer, the farmer would have sent for Annixter to come and drive them back where they belong. A hole in a fence, which must happen with certain regularity, would be only an irritation or distraction. The railroad, however, is without compromise or consideration of life, even bestial life. It slaughters sheep and then criticizes the farmer who allowed them to escape. In addition, the railroad is of such size that the man actually responsible for the slaughter, the engineer, is long since in some other part of the state. Annixter cannot accuse Behrman of killing them. Behrman merely represents the company. Thus the railroad is a new kind of neighbor the farmers must deal with, and they have little talent for it.

The scene remains with Annixter as the other three men leave him. The nonspecific bother and irritation which plague him are carried to extremes in the following pages, where he becomes jealous of Delany's apparent relationship with Hilma Tree. It should be clear to the reader that Annixter suffers from frustration and lack of human warmth, from lack of the love of a woman, and also that he does not himself understand what is bothering him. Although he is no longer an adolescent, his attitude toward Hilma Tree is immature and aggressive. He leaves for the Los Muertos Ranch in a fit of anger he does not understand. He wanted to show off and be admired by Hilma, but she appears to take no notice. While under the influence of his frustrated anger, he meets Delany and fires him with a flurry of verbal brutality.

The train passes like some spirit in the night, neither threatening nor brutal, but omnipresent. At the end of the first chapter, the train came through the valley like a wild animal, destroying sheep, destroying the poet's artistic imagination, and nearly killing the man himself. At the end of this chapter, the train shows its power by its omnipresence, rather than by its destructive force. The railroad, points out Norris, symbolically has both facets.

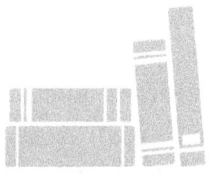

THE OCTOPUS

TEXTUAL ANALYSIS

BOOK I: CHAPTER THREE

....

At the ranchers' meeting in Magnus Derrick's house, the Bonneville newspaper editor suggests that the railroad will probably raise the price of the land to its current value before they make it available to the farmers. Two new characters, Broderson and Osterman, are introduced, and Osterman becomes very important by his persuasive plan to get control of the Railroad Commission through bribery. The farmers discuss the proposal, which represents a sharp departure from their usual manner of resistance, and find themselves divided on its merits.

COMMENT

The railroad owned alternate plots of land along their tracks as a land grant originally to help the industry get started, an historical fact. The company enticed settlers to the land by giving them an option to buy at some future date, after the settler had improved the land. The price, however, would remain at the original level before improvements had been made. There is no reason to assume that the original promises were not sincere. Once the company became enormous, they acquired the freedom and power to deny their original agreements, raise prices tenfold, and sell the land on a first-come, first-served basis. The first served, of course, would be a railroad man.

With Genslinger's suggestion that the railroad was about to grade the land and raise the price, the farmers found themselves suddenly locked in a battle not only for their livelihoods, but also for their possessions, their homes, their land. The groundwork that Norris has accomplished in the first two chapters allows the reader to feel with considerable force the identification of these farmers with their land. Somehow, the man and his land were a unity, and a threat to take away his land was like a threat to take away his life.

Presumably, Magnus Derrick called the meeting of ranchers in order to inform them of the failure of their court case in San Francisco and probably to hear suggestions for further action. He did not anticipate the news Genslinger brings about the grading of land, and he certainly did not expect the meeting to result in an organization of ranchers with specific intentions to act illegally or immorally against the railroad. Osterman, who proposes the bribery scheme, cannot be considered an evil man. He is morally average, as contrasted to Magnus's heroic espousal of moral integrity. There is no condemnation of either man in the tone of Norris's prose. Both men seem to be right, but Magnus is old-fashioned and not equipped to fight the new kind of power which corrupts, and Osterman is corrupted, as he must be in order to fight against the power.

Magnus Derrick will not immediately join the ranchers' organization because he cannot abide their methods. He is, of course, totally in sympathy with their objective, which is to influence the railroad to consider the needs of their patrons and inhibit the company's headlong rise to totalitarian power. The action proposed by Osterman is inevitable. The ranchers have Magnus in a tight corner, because he knows that he is their natural leader, because he cannot stand aside and allow the other farmers to abase themselves in order to accomplish a victory that would benefit him.

The courses of action open to the farmers are only two: to retreat, or to fight with tools morally unacceptable to Magnus. Of course, they fight. Magnus is not short-sighted. He can see the inevitable arrival of a compromise with his moral sense. A distinction can be drawn between Mrs. Derrick and Magnus at this point. Mrs. Derrick, by being unable to see the inevitability of the compromise, becomes merely a decoration, unessential to the events which happen in the story. Although Harran Derrick is not more intelligent than his father, he is more modern and more ready to admit that the railroad must be fought with weapons capable of inflicting damage, whether the weapons are moral or not.

The business of Chapter Three is rather weighty, and Norris eases the burden of it with a thread of comedy. Annixter inadvertently plays the buffoon for Osterman, who is normally a comic character. Annixter, who has brought his bad humor and aggressive attitude along with him to the meeting, resents the undignified name, Buck, which Osterman calls him in front of Mrs. Derrick. Hiding a pudding in his bed is a rather tasteless joke, but somehow affectionate. Despite his bitterness, Annixter is not hated by the other ranchers. In Chapter One when Presley spoke to Solotari in Guadalajara, the restaurant owner praised Annixter highly for his shrewdness and business sense.

The observation about Annixter is important because Norris wants to draw a clear line of demarcation between the kind of man who is a rancher and the kind of man who is a railroad man. Behrman, for example, has no desirable quality about him. Delany will become a far different person once he has been accepted into the fold of railroad men. Norris seems to be suggesting that the company squeezes the life out of human beings, even the human beings who are its agents and to whom it provides a living.

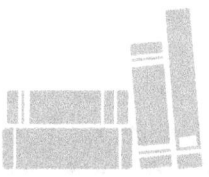

THE OCTOPUS

TEXTUAL ANALYSIS

BOOK I: CHAPTER FOUR

This chapter contains a long, **epic** scene of plowing on the Quien Sabe Ranch, and a description of the lives of the plow crews. Vanamee, who is driving a plow for Annixter, goes to the Mission and engages in a long discussion of God with Father Sarria. The priest retires and Vanamee attempts to comfort himself in the church. Unable to find solace there, he goes out to Angele's grave and calls to her with his mystical power. He imagines a faint response from somewhere, but returns exhausted to the Quien Sabe Ranch.

COMMENT

After the sunless and oppressive business of the previous chapter, the scenes which open Chapter Four are a great burst of sun, life, progress, fertility, and honest work. The scenes are much more that mere "local color." Norris is building the land into a force, an abstract power in the universe, stronger than the power of mere human beings, and stronger even than the power of any organization of human beings, such as the railroad. The earth is the source of fertility in the universe, the female principle of creation, birth, and growth. The men who ride the plows care for her with their machines, woo her, and fecundate her with seed.

The requirements of naturalism, which Norris represents, cause him to include scenes that may have been offensive to certain of his readers, readers with taste like Mrs. Derrick's. In Chapter Two, she was reading the "flaccid banalities of the 'Minor Poets'" and was shocked by the coarseness of Homer, who could not be literature, in her estimation. It is precisely this Homeric quality, the grandness of the Homeric canvas, with its great variety of characters, and its scenes ranging from the most coarse to the most delicate, that Norris is attempting to capture. He considered his work to be in the epic school of Homer. He felt that he was capturing the breadth of life in the raw, with great feeling and sympathy for it.

Vanamee, who dominates Chapter Four, is himself a mythical, Homeric character. His passions are grander than life, and his conduct is irrational and motivated by strange urges and compulsions that drive him to do things unheard of by "normal" men. He has the gift of a mystical power than can overcome the will of another man. At the mission he summons Father Sarria to him, profoundly disturbing the priest with the occult power. Vanamee as a character symbolizes the completely spiritual, nonphysical man. He longs, however, for the physical presence of his lost Angele, unable to accept a substitute for her. For Norris, the character of Vanamee has philosophical bearing on the doctrine of naturalism. The physical power of objects, of human beings, and of human contact are a fundamental assumption of naturalism. The physicality of "things" alters the life and the meaning of life for the people who are surrounded by them. Vanamee is only one-half a man, the spiritual half, during this scene. Annixter, by contrast, is a totally physical man at this point in the novel. Later on, when Vanamee accepts Angele's daughter in place of Angele, he becomes a whole man. And when Annixter recognizes his love for Hilma Tree, he too becomes a total man. At this juncture, however, neither man can foresee his future completeness. Vanamee wants Father Sarria's God to make a physical demonstration of His existence. Vanamee cannot be satisfied with the belief that he will encounter his beloved as a spirit in heaven when he too will be a spirit.

After the priest has gone to bed, Vanamee acts out the compulsion that drives him. He calls for Angele with his mystical power. He tried to find consolation by the Christian road recommended by Father Sarria, and found that he did not believe. It does not matter in any larger sense to the reader whether Vanamee is a madman or a fool. He is sincere, which says more about him than any long list of adjectives. He does want he learns he must do when he looks into himself and asks the question: what must I do? Some faint response comes to him from somewhere, surprising him perhaps more than the reader.

This chapter about Vanamee may seem to be very far afield from the troubles that plague the ranchers and their fight against the power of the railroad. The main criticism Norris lodges against the railroad is its total lack of consideration for human life or happiness when confronted with the profit motive. Love and kindness are totally absent, totally subverted to the desire for power and profit. The absence of love and consideration in human affairs is deadly and brutalizing, according to Norris. He shows that contention through both Vanamee and Annixter. Vanamee has not been brutalized by the loss of Angele, but part of him has been killed. Annixter, on the other hand, is bitter and brutalized by the absence of love in his life. When he finally allows love to become a power in his life, Annixter blooms like a beautiful flower, changing from an undesirable character to a man of great tenderness.

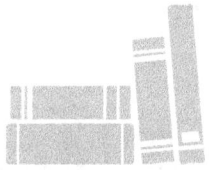

THE OCTOPUS

TEXTUAL ANALYSIS

BOOK I: CHAPTER FIVE

Annixter receives notification from Osterman that one candidate For the Railroad Commission has been engaged. As he departs for Los Muertos, his interest is taken by the beauty of Hilma Tree and he makes an improper advance toward her, which results only in confusion and humiliation. At Los Muertos, Annixter attempts to enlist Magnus in the ranchers' organization, but Mrs. Derrick sways Magnus away. Failing, Annixter leaves with Presley and they meet Harran at Caraher's Saloon. Harran, only a silent partner, is prepared to come actively into the organization, despite the tension between his fidelity to his father and his desire to help the cause. Annixter continues to Bonneville and faces the P. and S. W. on the issue of land grading, without success. Dyke verifies the cost of hops shipments, and then sneaks away to the railroad controlled bank to mortgage his belongings and crop. After lunching with Father Sarria, Annixter unsuccessfully tries to smooth things over with Hilma Tree and finally falls asleep, with his mind engaged by a dream.

COMMENT

Chapter Five is an important day in Annixter's life, a day during which he pushes forward his interests on two fronts. Soon after he arises, he receives the note, expressed in a code so that the railroad men who run the telegraph office cannot understand it, that Osterman has succeeded in engaging the services of one representative for the ranchers' organization. The note clearly states that bribery money will be needed to pay the representative. At this time, the ranchers' organization numbers only Annixter, Broderson, Osterman, and Harran, as a silent partner. The first of his interests to be advanced this day is the ranchers' organization. The direction and method of operation have been set by Osterman's success. A commitment has been made. The second of Annixter's interests to be advanced this day is the beginning of his romance with Hilma Tree. The masculine and slightly oppressive atmosphere of Annixter's house contrasts sharply with Norris's description of Hilma Tree working in the dairy house. Annixter's unnamed and, to him, unknown source of irritation begins to take focus on Hilma Tree as he realizes that he is strongly attracted to her. He is accustomed to ignoring women and ridiculing their powers of attraction. Completely without experience, he does not know how to conduct himself. By trying to kiss her, he of course offends her, and in his confusion does not know how to smooth over the affront. He speaks to her as if she were an excited animal, and storms away in a fit of humiliation. Annixter is not brutal in his attitude toward Hilma, but he does not know how to express tenderness. A whole new area of life is painfully awakening in Annixter, the area which will be the most rewarding in his life. The awakening of his new sense of other people is clearly shown by the interest in preparing properly for the barn party. He wants the proper invitations to be sent out, and of course he does not know how to conduct that social business until he discusses it with Presley and Mrs. Derrick.

The conflict between the farmers' obvious need for his services and the need to compromise with his ingrained principles put an enormous strain on Magnus. He knows that eventually he will have to fail. Mrs. Derrick does not understand that her husband is in a trap which slowly closes about him. Thematically Norris is showing the inevitability of Magnus's destruction. The power of the railroad to corrupt a man of the "old politics" is ineluctable. By "old politics" Norris means to differentiate between statesmanship and politics, the former conducted according to principles of honor and trust, and the latter a form of opportunism.

Tension also weighs heavily on Harran Derrick. He wants to remain faithful to his father, but at the same time he knows that he must join the farmers' resistance organization and subscribe to their methods of operation, even if contrary to his sense of moral action.

As if again to satisfy the reader that the railroad is not honorable, Norris shows in the next scene that the company does not act in good faith. Annixter attempts to force the issue of the price of his land. The man he deals with cannot make any decisions. The railroad is a bureaucracy where a petty official does not have the power to alter the course of his company's action. The net result of trying to do business with the land agent is humiliation for Annixter. He can get no satisfaction whatsoever. In addition, the agent is shown to have various habits, like his incessant doodling and jotting, which tend to reduce the reader's estimation of him. He is only a mouthpiece, himself caught in the web of oppression and destruction which his company represents. He has no identity separate from the

P. and S. W. Men like him and Behrman are very sad people, without humanity, love, or the spirit of generosity. They represent the company line of oppression and the drive for wealth at the expense of all other values.

Contrasted to the land agent and Behrman is Dyke, who was at one time a representative of the railroad. When he comes into the office to check on the price for shipping hops, he is like a new man whose life is just opening before him. Contact with the soil, a project which depends on his own skill, understanding, and diligence, with a chance of great success, will soon make him over into a different man. It will be as if a new portion of him wakes up and begins to express itself. Before, however, he can begin the new life based on his own manhood, he must mortgage himself - his land and his crops - to the railroad for money. He senses the humiliation involved and sneaks into the office, hoping that his friends will not see him.

Father Sarria must represent Christian ethics, Christian love, and Christian morality in this novel. In the scene where he launches with Annixter and his basket is shown to contain two fighting cocks, Norris is making a gentle, somewhat comical criticism of the force of Christianity in the Valley. Earlier, when Vanamee visited with Father Sarria, the priest was unable to uphold the Christian point of view to the mystic. The priest is ineffectual in the affairs of men and is himself a twister of the truth. Although the scene with his basket of fighting cocks is comic, it nevertheless shows the priest seriously at fault. Father Sarria did after all misrepresent the truth to Annixter, and did conduct himself in such a way that his exposure caused him humiliation. In his conversation with Annixter, Father Sarria mentions that he has few people in his congregation, and most of them Mexicans. The good father is a sympathetic character, but without moral force. His kindness and good nature fit him well, but they do not influence others.

The **theme** of the earth's fecund power as a force in the universe and the lives of men is advanced in the chapter where Annixter, on his way to Magnus's house, stops to watch the thirty-three grain drills pass by planting the newly plowed soil. It is an almost primeval power which Norris evokes, a power which remains unaffected by the passing of centuries and civilizations, essentially unchanged by the invention of machinery and the sophistication of cultivation techniques. It is the power of creation itself, symbolized by the growing of grain. Presley's artistic grasp of his **epic** poem in Chapter One is generated by the influence of the earth on his imagination. The nefarious influence of the railroad, perverting and exploiting the products of the earth, is analogous to the nefarious influence of the company on individual men, making them all into men like Behrman, and, as the reader later sees, into men like Dyke and like Magnus, who are broken and destroyed by the company. It is the passing of the locomotive which wipes out Presley's artistic vision at the end of Chapter One, and it is the mystic Vanamee who is described riding on the plow in Chapter Two. Norris identifies them both as artists, as poets, and they both have this special analogous relationship with the earth.

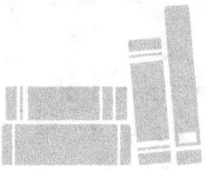

THE OCTOPUS

TEXTUAL ANALYSIS

BOOK I: CHAPTER SIX

While launching together in Guadalajara, Vanamee describes to Presley the strange response he has received to his mystical summoning at the Mission. The two poets stop at Dyke's new ranch to visit his family and learn that Dyke will not join the ranchers' organization. They continue to Annixter's ranch, finding party preparations in full swing. The flurry of preparation ends as Annixter, who has been confused by his desire to befriend Hilma Tree, welcomes the first carry-all load of party guests. The ranchers closet themselves in the harness room to drink punch and tell stories while the other guests dance. The gaiety is suddenly shattered by the entrance of Delany mounted on the buckskin. After a few drunken words from Delany, he and Annixter fire at each other, and Delany is hit. He disappears and the party gets underway again. The alcohol is having its effect on the ranchers when a messenger arrives from Bonneville bearing a letter from the P. and S. W. to each of the ranchers.

Their lands have been graded at the highest possible figures and their option rights have been dropped. The party immediately changes into a political meeting. A League is formed and Magnus joins as its leader. The guests drift off into the night under the burden of foreboding events.

COMMENT

Vanamee and Presley are unable to come to any definitive explanation for the meaning of Vanamee's night experiences in the Mission yard. Vanamee, the "natural poet," as Norris calls him, feels compelled to push himself into the realm of the unknown. His whole appearance and manner seem to require him to exercise the gift that is his alone. Presley, the "trained poet," has sufficient scope of imagination to understand that Vanamee is moving into an area forbidden to other men. Their conversation is necessary to Vanamee, but not to Presley, who is only a spectator to the events at this time. Later, of course, Vanamee will bequeath to Presley the lessons he learns from his experience.

Dyke is a relatively happy man when the two poets visit him, but he is divided between bitterness toward the railroad and an attitude of trust toward the company. They have a mortgage on his whole holdings, and they have quoted him a price for shipment of his hops which will allow him to make a large sum of money. His future is completely in the company's hands. The reader can sense a slight stain of pride in Dyke's attitude when he repeats that he is going to make a lot of money. He is not, however, actually greedy. He wants merely to take care of his family properly and get some security in his life. This scene with Dyke is especially warm and pleasantly suffused with the gentler human emotions. He is an open and somewhat childish man whom one instinctively likes. He works hard and has modest tastes and ambitions, except perhaps for his dream of having a lot of money.

The long and detailed description of the party, with its elaborate preparations and enormous attendance, is one of the most interesting and informative **episodes** in the book. The details of decorations, costumes, and manners are essentially accurate and inherently interesting for what they tell the reader about the American West of the period just after the frontier days, when the first rays of European and native American cultures were making themselves felt. Stylistically, Norris does an excellent job with this difficult scene. He shows close-up portraits of certain people and then draws back and communicates the sense of the whole atmosphere. He then comes in close to another individual or group of individuals and points out details of conduct. Throughout the whole scene he keeps up the back-and-forth movement of his perspective, much the way a movie camera would record such a scene.

On this day, the relationship between Annixter and Hilma Tree begins to crystalize as a positive force. When the two face each other in the barn before the party, Annixter is not nearly as dumb and confused as he has been in the past when facing her. He has begun to realize that she is a human being requiring intelligent conduct on his part, and that his attraction to her is a desirable and important part of his life. He is not completely coherent, of course, when he tells her that he wants her to like him because he wants everybody to like him. Annixter is not a man of great articulation or verbal suavity. The moment of real communication between them is silent, a mere glance which tells them both what they could not put in words for each other.

The various ranchers have this occasion to be together in a situation which reveals sides of their personalities other than their serious, business involvements with each other. The men have robust senses of humor and a kind of mutual regard that expresses itself in teasing, practical jokes, and tall tales. They are shy of women and have little sophistication, or little of that Latin gaiety expressed through self-dramatization, like dancing or singing together. They are very American in their lack of formality but not total absence of reserve. Norris is not completely innocent of **satire** as he draws the lighter sides of the ranchers' personalities.

There are many humorous passages in this party scene. The young man who shaves candles on the floor is an example of a humorous figure introduced merely to emphasize the gaiety of the event. For humor Norris usually concentrates on fine points of human conduct, tracing the vagaries of manners among people. Hooven repeats his one funny joke about "vertilizer" all evening long, while Osterman, who begins by playing the political operator, soon returns to his original character as a buffoon.

The arrival of Delany on the buckskin jars the party into a new and solemn event. It may perhaps be difficult for the reader to believe Norris's presentation of the gunfight between Annixter and Delany. Its drama and excitement, however, are not out of character with the time and location in which the novel takes place. The element of violence, brutality, and great force lurking beneath the surface of apparent gentility is a common **theme** of naturalism. Such sudden and inconvenient contrasts are not inconsistent with life. Delany, it seems certain, is motivated by pride and aided by alcohol, which allows his more reckless conduct to take control of him.

Arrival of the letters from the railroad announcing the grading of the land is a powerful blow to the farmers and catches them when their resistance is lowered by alcohol and good spirits. The change that comes over them, metamorphosing joviality into panic, is an important **theme** of naturalist writers, not unrelated to the naturalist **theme** mentioned in the previous paragraph. Naturalists often wanted to show that the spectrum of the human personality contains many parts ranging from the tenderest gentleness to the most vicious selfishness and lack of control. Circumstances, or environment, are capable of causing human beings to assume various parts of their personality. In the case at hand, Magnus is persuaded to compromise his principles to take on the leadership of the newly formed League. He realizes that he has no other course of action if he is to remain a leader of men, a role he feels himself destined to play.

The end of Book One closes with a chilling comment by Vanamee, to whom the reader is expected to assign more than common powers of foresight, that the ranchers will fail, will meet their Waterloo. The whole development of Book One has been the process of aligning the farmers together as a single unit and expression of power pitted against the railroad power. At the end of this book, the two forces are facing each other and the terms of the fight are known to each. The letters have apprised the farmers of the company's complete disavowal of their previous commitments. The fight will be a free-for-all power showdown.

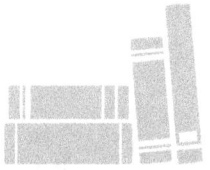

THE OCTOPUS

TEXTUAL ANALYSIS

BOOK II: CHAPTER ONE

Lyman Derrick, Magnus's other son who is a lawyer in San Francisco, has been elected to the Railroad Commission. The League has two bribed representatives on the Commission, and has given them instructions to resist the railroad's land takeover and to regulate the wheat rates in favor of the farmers. Progress of the League through the winter is described. The United States Circuit Court is about to hand down a decision on a case testing the railroad's rights to ignore their original commitments. Presley, Magnus, and Harran go up to San Francisco to be present. San Francisco society is introduced to the reader at Lyman Derrick's club, where Cedarquist conducts a lively discussion of American culture and business as many prominent San Francisco types march before the reader, presenting a satirical picture of America's supper classes. The idea of selling wheat in the Orient catches Magnus's imagination, but the fantasy is quickly dispelled by the court's decision in favor of the railroad.

COMMENT

Lyman Derrick's environment, being urban, is sharply in contrast to the environment of his father and brother. His actual goals are vastly different, since they include gaining political power over other men and exploiting the position to acquire wealth. In a way, Lyman is carrying on the aspiration of his father, but Lyman is in the "new politics" rather than the "old," represented by his father. The father's goal in the "old" days was leadership for the good of the people rather than power over people for the purpose of self-aggrandizement. In the "new politics" the means of acquiring power is rather opportunistic and of such a nature that a candid revelation of a candidate's alliances and opinions would be a definite humiliation. All through this chapter, there is a constant contrast between the dignity of the father and the pragmatism of the son. Norris is not overly simplistic, however, in his portrayals of the two politicians. Magnus, although an "old politician," has a complex motivation which includes a great deal of ego and selfishness. The difference Norris wants to point out is that the "old politician" was guided by an innate moral sense that prohibited him from exploiting his political position. The reader can sense no such moral attitude in Lyman.

One notable exception to the dignified presentation of Magnus's character occurs in the discussion between him and his son about regulating the wheat rates. Lyman suggests that if the present Railroad Commission succeeds in putting the rates down, the next Commission might well raise them. Magnus says that it would not matter because, "We would have made our fortunes by then." The sentiment appears to be inconsistent with Magnus's character. It bears out a **theme** of the naturalist writers as to the fundamental nature of man, even great and exceptional men like Magnus Derrick. Beneath the surface of cultivation and finer sentiments exists a strain of selfishness and a desire to acquire wealth and power. Under the wrong circumstances, these darker and less desirable tendencies will bloom, according to the naturalist point of view. The darker tendencies are quite strong in Lyman, and seem to be getting stronger in Magnus. Norris wants the reader to understand the change that is coming about as the result of the railroad monopoly, the techniques big business uses to spread their power and the kind of conduct necessary to fight it. The reader knows, of course, that Magnus has compromised his principles to stoop to bribery. However, the hoped for result will benefit a vast number of people. The compromise is not done merely to benefit Magnus, although he will be one of the people who will benefit from its success.

The element of human bestiality is always present, and certain circumstances bring it to the surface in subtle ways. The San Francisco society drawn in the scene in the Club has certain trappings of great elegance and refinement, but the moral situation of the society is exemplified by a man like Lyman. The industrialist Cedarquist is an exception to that frivolous society. He has principles and a certain serious turn of mind. Cedarquist realizes that money, power, and appearances have the strongest influence. He is irate that San Francisco businessmen will spend a million dollars on the Million Dollar Fair and Flower Festival, a "gingerbread fete," while allowing a steel plant to languish from lack of funds. The factory would be useful, productive, give jobs and provide material for construction and so on. But, it apparently is not showy enough for the businessmen to be interested. Norris writes with a certain amount of bitterness when he draws the character of San Francisco society. He uses **satire**, ridicule, and **irony** in order to communicate his understanding of the failure of that society. He considers these people frivolous, blind to the serious problems which surround them, opportunistic, and unaffected by the force of morality. Cedarquist, the exception, says that the greatest evil in American life is public indifference to public affairs. Contrasted to his serious involvement with important questions is the satirical scene of "art lovers" making ridiculous judgments of Hatrath's painting and comparing it to the work of European artists. Mrs. Cedarquist is satirized for her frivolous championship of the various "fakes" who show up to milk the rich for a parasitical living - decayed musicians, religious fanatics, prestidigitators, exotic characters from the East, and so on. Mrs. Cedarquist is not alone in her occupation with those characters. The whole upper crust of San Francisco adopts them for a while before moving on to another amusement.

Against the backdrop of such frivolity, a fight to the death is going on between a giant corporation and a band of farmers. Blood will flow. Men and families will be crushed and maimed by the conflict, but the blasé surface of gentility will go on as before, unruffled by the horror right outside their windows.

During the winter the League has consolidated its strength under the leadership of Magnus Derrick. Their two delegates, secretly bribed by Magnus, have been seated on the Commission. They have cleared away previous business and started to carry out the program requested by the ranchers. A test case was tried and lost in local court and is in appeal to the U.S. Circuit Court, where the farmers feel confident of a decision of their favor - despite the power of Shelgrim over the workings of justice in the state.

The **irony** of Chapter One comes to its fine point at the very end, when the farmers learn that they have lost their case. At the moment when their hopes are utterly dashed, Mrs. Cedarquist rushes into the room, screaming with excitement that she has won the Hatrath painting in a raffle. The triumph of the frivolous!

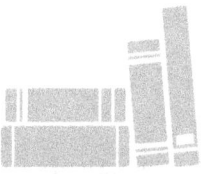

THE OCTOPUS

TEXTUAL ANALYSIS

BOOK II: CHAPTER TWO

....

Annixter and Hilma meet under the best of circumstances for them to communicate with each other. They manage to declare their love and all seems well until Annixter says that he is not the marrying kind of man. Hilma, who had understood his declaration of love to be a proposal of marriage, runs away terrified. Dyke, whose hops have progressed well, is shown living a busy but quietly joyful life with his mother and daughter. He travels to Bonneville one day to conduct some business and stops off at the railroad office to notify the company that he will need cars to carry his hops. He learns that the rate has been raised from two cents to five. He is wiped out by the price hike. Stunned, he wanders through Bonneville telling the story to everyone, including Caraher, the anarchist, at his saloon, where Presley overhears the conversation. Annixter returns to his ranch to discover that Hilma and her family have gone away. Annixter agonizes through the night until his crude self-awareness finally allows him to realize that he loves the girl. The light of dawn reveals to him that the wheat has pushed up through the ground.

COMMENT

When Annixter and Hilma meet along the edge of the creek, they are both under the romantic influence of the location. The slow and agonized process of self-awareness that has been working inside each of them, especially Annixter, finally finds an outlet in an inarticulate and unaware declaration of love. Hilma understands in her nonintellectual way and returns the emotion. Annixter has not actually realized what he is doing by making a declaration of love or what it means to him. He has advanced very far from his original position of scorning women. He can scarcely imagine going any farther, certainly not as far as marriage. He is not averse to marriage. It is merely that he has not thought that far ahead. He does not have designs to corrupt Hilma or use her for his convenience. He is utterly sincere as far as his understanding takes him.

It is essential to realize that Annixter does not have ulterior motives, because his process of coming to awareness about love is one of the most moving and satisfying motifs in the novel. The reader need only remember Annixter's mental condition in the first and second chapters to realize that he has solved the basic emotional problem of his life by falling in love. Love, however, has its responsibilities. It requires commitment and the change of certain habits, which he resists.

When he wanders out on the land at night to brood through to an understanding of himself, there is a certain parallel to Vanamee's brooding in the Mission yard at night. Both men are taken over by the emotion of love. Although Vanamee is at present frustrated by his love, since Angele is dead, Annixter is just realizing what kind of responsibilities are required of him as a result of his love. Hilma has forced his hand by rushing away to San Francisco. He must decide whether to follow and take her to him, or whether to ignore her departure and carry on as before.

He realizes that she brings out in him all of the gentler and more masculine traits, like the desire to provide for a woman and to establish a family. He comes to his realization just as the dawn lights up the valley and he can see that the wheat has poked through the surface of the ground. Norris is drawing a parallel between the man choosing in favor of love and family and the fertility of the great earth force. The nonartistic creative process in the universe is manifest in man when he joins the natural scheme of things and emulates the fecundity of earth by taking wife and propagating his kind. The love, the joining of two people, and the creation of family are the route dictated by nature as the way for man to emulate the best force in nature, the force of creation, the support of life.

Counterpointed to Annixter's emotional breakthrough is Dyke's emotional breakdown as the natural result of unnatural human behavior. The railroad has raised the price of hops transport so high, out of a profit motive without regard for human values, that Dyke cannot survive no matter how hard he works his land. The bank has a mortgage on his property and crop, and it must be paid. He cannot pay. Dyke is not a complex of scheming man. He is open, simple, capable of great happiness or great anger without intellectual understanding of either. He has been betrayed a second time by the company and they have not even courtesy enough to make an excuse. Behrman tells him that the railroad sets fares according to what the traffic will bear. Dyke knows only that all of his plans for his daughter and mother are impossible, even if he were to work himself to the bone. The knowledge is more than he can bear. He is swept under by the awful consequences of betrayal.

The profit motive, suggests Norris, when allowed to acquire monopolistic power, loses its regard for human beings and becomes a machine of destruction. The reader should differentiate between the profit motive as exhibited by Magnus and the profit motive as exhibited by the P. and S. W. Magnus is restrained by a sense of fair play. He could not betray and destroy a man as the company betrays Dyke. In addition, Magnus and the other farmers are fighting to establish claims to their land. They have no halfway mark. If they fail to establish the claim, they will be evicted and left with nothing.

Norris wrote the scene with Dyke in the P. and S. W. office very carefully, to illustrate the attitude of the company. They not only betray a man, but they do it insolently. At the same time, they become defensive and unpleasant if they have to spend any of their accumulated wealth. The man who brings in the automatic door opener is subjected to abuse because he requires the company to purchase a sign to accompany the opener.

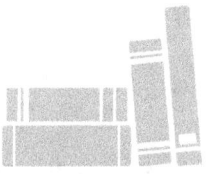

THE OCTOPUS

TEXTUAL ANALYSIS

BOOK II: CHAPTER THREE

Hearing Dyke's story while at Caraher's Saloon, Presley is outraged and his anger takes form in a poem, "The Toilers," which he has begun earlier without a clear idea of what he wanted to say. The insight comes to him and he writes. To judge the poem he seeks out Vanamee, who pronounces it "great." Vanamee leaves their meeting and goes to the Mission. On the way he passes the brooding figure of Annixter, who is fighting through to a self-realization of his love for Hilma. Vanamee, the man whose love is so profound that he cannot adjust to the death of his woman, calls out to her spirit in the Mission yard, as is his nightly habit. The woman appears as Angele's daughter and Vanamee has found again the women he loves. As dawn comes, Vanamee-like Annixter-sees the valley turned green by the rising wheat.

COMMENT

This night is a time of great creation and growth. The man who did not know that he was in love comes to know it. The man whose love has been warped by the loss of his love object acquires another who is the same in his eyes. The artist creates his poem. The wheat which has been germinating in the soil pushes through to the surface, changing the barren brown earth to a delicate green. All of the events are related in some way, at least thematically, in the view of the author of the novel. It is a day when the principle of natural development has been in power for these men. Contrasted to them, of course, is Dyke, who is spending his first night in the full knowledge that his life, which had been until that day rewarding and fulfilling, is now destroyed.

Norris was of the opinion that a literary work must have a message, as he explained in his book of essays, *The Responsibilities of a Novelist*. He transfers that conviction to Presley and shows the reader how Presley, aroused by his sense of social wrong, is driven to artistic utterance. Vanamee pronounces the poem "great" because it sincerely presents a message, "the truth." The poem, although never quoted for the reader, obviously contains a message, that is, an idea, which in some general way probably communicates the sense of social wrong which Dyke's experience illustrates. The poem most likely communicates the very ideas of social justice, human responsibility, and human exploitation which *The Octopus* itself succeeds in communicating.

Vanamee advises Presley not to publish the poem in a literary magazine because there it would be read only by people interested in literature. The message would be lost to the people for whom it has importance, the people, the vulgus. Vanamee is stating another of Norris's convictions about literature. It must be common and of the people. It must communicate its message directly to those who have need of the social insight the author has achieved. Therefore, the proper vehicle is the newspaper and, of course, Presley resolves to submit it to a newspaper. The idea expressed by this approach to literature is anti-romantic to the extent that the author of the poem remains secondary to the idea contained in the poem. In most romantic work the author of the poem is also the subject of it. Not so with "The Toilers," nor with Norris's idea of the proper social use of art and literature. In addition, the audience for great, serious, romantic literature was usually a restricted group of people who sought out poetry as an artistic experience, rather than as a social experience. In other words, Mrs. Cedarquist and her circle of effete friends would read the poem if it were published in a literary magazine, rather than the people whose lives the poem would really touch.

The **irony** of the society scenes in Chapter One (Book Two) can perhaps be seen more clearly by the reader now that Norris has explicitly expressed his point of view toward art. Hatrath's painting could not be considered a serious contribution to the fundamental issues of life, in Norris's opinion. It is a mere pretty scene for the amusement of bored people looking for a new fad-like a Russian countess with dirty fingernails.

The source of the answer to Vanamee's summons to Angele is finally revealed to be her daughter, also named Angele. It is not difficult to understand how Angele the daughter is in some way Angele the mother. They are of the same flesh and the same blood. The one came from the other, as if the mother had passed her life on down into a new, pure body. And, it seems obvious, Vanamee's conviction makes the identity certain. The reader must realize that Vanamee is a mystic and that he lives by guidelines not circumscribed by the dictates of logic.

The reader should also notice how Norris relates the flower garden to Angele. In some way she comes forth out of the field of flowers. In this scene, flowers must be understood not only as the embodiment of natural beauty, but also as the vessel and vehicle of reproduction and creation in nature. The flower contains the seed that produces the new generation. The flower is the sign, like wheat, of the creative force of earth and nature, a sign of the fertility of nature, and an illustration of the great feat of natural law to cause generation after generation to come forth on the earth. With men, such a law is obeyed in the taking of wife, the loving, the bringing forth of new life, and the supporting of it. The human endeavor should be the emulation of earth, the support and cherishing of life.

The P. and S. W. railroad in its dealings so far with the farmers does not conform to this great natural injunction. It destroys life in the San Joaquin Valley. The reader should be cautioned at this point, however, to be careful in his judgment of the railroad. He will soon see that from a larger point of view, the railroad may not be so hostile to life. Much of the vitality of Norris's novel comes expressly from the dual role of the railroad as destroyer and supporter of life.

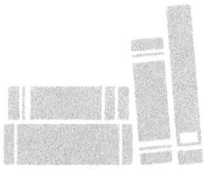

THE OCTOPUS

TEXTUAL ANALYSIS

BOOK II: CHAPTER FOUR

While Presley achieves a certain fame from *his* poem, Dyke's life quickly decays. Even Magnus Derrick is beginning to crumble under the pressure of his moral compromise. Annixter's life is reaching a point of fruition. He goes to San Francisco and marries Hilma Tree. As they are returning to Bonneville, Dyke holds up the train and kills one of the guards. He becomes a fugitive pursued like a wild animal by several possies. Annixter takes care of Dyke's family. The League meets in executive session to inspect the new scale of rates secured by their representative on the Railroad Commission. Lyman Derrick comes down from San Francisco to present the rates. He has clearly not carried out his responsibilities, and the farmers, aware of the betrayal, drive him away. Magnus disowns him.

COMMENT

Chapter Four continues to illustrate the life destroying force of the railroad power over the farmers in the San Joaquin Valley. The decay advances. A mother loses her son to animal brutality and a father loses his son to betrayal and treachery. Only Annixter and Presley advance in a positive direction during the time covered in this chapter.

Annixter carries out an unusual but proper courtship of Hilma Tree and they get married in San Francisco. After a short honeymoon, they buy new furniture and household articles for the Quien Sabe Ranch. There is a certain ceremonial establishment-of-the-household involved in the elaborate purchases made by Annixter and Hilma. It is as though the creation of a new family required the establishment of a new house, a new environment. The reader is never allowed to feel real joy at the consummation of Annixter's love, because Norris breaks their love story with the horror story of Dyke's revenge against the railroad.

Dyke becomes an animal lashing out with savage cruelty at the company. One man alone can do nothing against the vast power of the railroad. His attack is totally beside the point since the money he steals does not strike at the heart of the power and the man he kills is a simple employee who does not deserve the violence. However, in his simple frustration, Dyke lashes out and is suddenly turned into a wild animal with a price on his head, pursued into the mountains by armed possies. Dyke has abandoned everything in his life that was important to him, especially his family. The desertion of Dyke's family has symbolical meaning in the chapter. While Annixter establishes a family, Dyke is forced to abandon his, and Magnus loses a son from his.

Irony attends the establishment of Annixter's family. The first packing case he opens at the house after his return with his bride contains a dozen Winchester rifles. Beneath the current of positive life-giving development in the novel, there exists always the threat to peace and happiness of the life-destroying power of the railroad.

The meeting of the League at Magnus's house is an important scene in the novel. There, Norris shows how the corruptive force of the profit motive uncontained by moral guidelines turns son against father. Lyman Derrick has the suavity and insincere slickness of a "new" politician, pleasing people, acting interested, spouting fixed phrases, obscuring the point with over-complex language. The farmers show a kind of shrewdness, notably Annixter, who because of Hilma suddenly has a new and very large responsibility to protect his home.

Norris is showing how the force of the railroad makes continual subtle inroads on the happiness and well-being of the farmers. Magnus, caught in a trap, is forced to resort to bribery. The mere fact of having submitted to the "new" politics saps something from his character. Some subtle element is gone from his personality, some element that affects his self-respect and confidence.

Dyke, of course, has acted the only way he knows how, directly and without bribery, like a caged beast. Lyman is corrupted by the company. Their power can make his ambitions come true. He cannot resist aligning himself with the powerful side, even though it requires betraying his own family. It is this corruption that creeps into men's lives, transforming the simple pursuit of happiness and well-being into a complicated and difficult enterprise with its numerous pressures too powerful to avoid.

The last paragraph in the chapter helps the reader understand how Norris conceived the force of wheat, and indirectly the creative force of the earth, to be an uncommitted, nonhuman power that remains unaffected by the vicissitudes of men. The wheat is a force of good, a force of creation, but it has no moral existence. The appearance of the wheat is good, since it eventually ends up as bread on the tables of hungry people. Wheat does not share guilt for the crimes which it inspires among men. Nature does not know immorality. It is only man who is capable of immorality. A man killed Angele. Men are corrupted by the urge to profit from what the earth brings forth for all men.

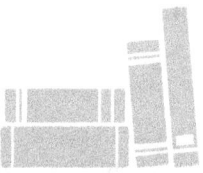

THE OCTOPUS

TEXTUAL ANALYSIS

BOOK II: CHAPTER FIVE

....

Genslinger, the newspaper editor, blackmails Magnus Derrick by holding publication of the bribery story over his head. The two Railroad Commissioners have apparently confessed to him as a representative of the railroad power. The farmers practice military drill to prepare for a showdown of force with the railroad, while rumors of the League's illegal methods begin to weaken the ranks of the farmers. Annixter, preparing for a picnic with his wife and Dyke's family, receives a sudden visit from Dyke, who in fleeing is only a few minutes in front of the posse. After a wild and futile chase the ex-engineer and hops farmer is taken like the savage animal he has become.

COMMENT

Once the League has committed itself to an illegal or questionable course of action, the railroad has a lever to bring clandestine pressure to bear on the farmers. In his characteristically thorough way, Genslinger has ferreted out the facts about the League's bribery scheme, presumably from the two bribed commissioners themselves. Certainly it is not difficult to believe that Lyman Derrick would tell the organization all that he knew, once the farmers had found him out and turned against him.

Genslinger's crime is all the more terrible because he is a journalist, a profession traditionally dedicated to supporting right and exposing wrong in the community. A journalist is traditionally thought of as a privileged citizen in the community, a man whose word has weight and whose publication sets a pace in the community. Genslinger is an arm of the railroad power, on the one hand, and also a criminal in his own right. There is no reason to believe that the blackmail money will end up in the hands of the railroad. The crime was personal. Norris is showing yet another illustration of the way corruption grows to encompass the entire conduct of a man, once he is tainted.

As a naturalist, Norris subscribed to the theory that the capability for evil exists in all men. The force of environment is the controlling factor in a man's life, determining whether he will resist the elements of evil in his makeup or whether he will surrender and commit himself to that evil. The enormous power of the railroad gives the company freedom to conduct itself in any way it wants. It is guided by the profit motive and the desire to expand its power. In addition, the source of power is secreted in a building in San Francisco, far from the outlying areas where the company makes contact with the people. The men in the field receive orders from the central location. They have no power in themselves and no ability to give satisfaction to an irate patron. The railroad thus itself creates an environment that supports the growth of evil in men.

The League gets some of its strength and solidarity from a belief that they represent a moral resistance to the immoral expansion of the railroad. Once rumors begin to leak out that perhaps the League is using the same techniques as the railroad, the simple farmers begin to waver in their conviction. They begin to lose part of their motivation when their self-respect as members of the organization is weakened. The experience of the League is very similar to the experience of its leader, Magnus, whose strength is sapped by his loss of self-respect.

In the conversation between Presley and Annixter just before they are to leave on the picnic, Annixter speaks the moral point of view that Norris advocates. Annixter says that in the past he "never dreamed of anybody else" but himself. When he realized that he loved Hilma, his attitude changed. He began to see that human beings are all in the same world with problems enough. "A fellow can't live for himself any more than he can live by himself. He's got to think of others." He must think for men who are not capable. He must pay for people without money. In other words, a man has a social responsibility to other men. He must help. The inequality of men, Norris the naturalist would say, comes from chance. Chance makes one man more intelligent, another man richer. To possess wealth or talent above other men does not make a man more free, as might appear on the surface, but gives him more responsibilities and curtails his freedom.

Annixter has arrived at a sort of crude enlightenment. The beauty of it is its absolute simplicity-honesty and regard for others. At the very moment when the reader is treated to Annixter's statement of a moral position, Dyke enters the picture as a destroyed man just living out the last agonized hours of his life. He is an outlaw, but he has gained no advantage from it. He is pursued and hunted like an animal. One's sympathy remains with Dyke, despite his crimes, because the reader has known him at a time when he lived by Annixter's simple philosophy. Somewhere under the savagery of the man lies the same knowledge that Annixter has spoken. Circumstances have driven it out of sight.

THE OCTOPUS

TEXTUAL ANALYSIS

BOOK II: CHAPTER SIX

....

Even though the threat of forcible possession hangs over the farmers, they get together for a jackrabbit drive, a social event including nearly every farmer in the valley, much like Annixter's barn dance. While the farmers are enjoying their feast of fresh rabbit, word comes that the railroad men have moved into the Quien Sabe Ranch and were moving into the others. The six hundred Leaguers decline to get into the fight. Eleven farmers led by Magnus prepare to face the eleven railroad men, including a U.S. Marshall. The two groups confront each other and argue. A chance accident alarms the nervous farmers and sets off a gunfight. Two railroad men are killed, and so are Hooven, Dabney, and Annixter. Harran Derrick, Osterman, and Broderson are seriously wounded.

| Comment

The rabbit drive is a frontier social event which brings the whole community together. It plays an important role in this novel since its grandness is **epic** in the way Norris wanted his novel to contain a kind of Homeric grandeur. He wanted to seize not only characters and events concerning the wheat farmers in California, but also the spirit of the place. As in the story of Annixter's barn dance, the rabbit drive has humor, **satire**, and violence.

As in the previous social event, Hooven provides an often repeated humorous line about himself. He wants to shoot rabbits, but the marshal won't let him, according to Presley. Hooven is himself a marshal. Norris's **satire** is very gentle. He keeps it gentle by his genuine appreciation of people's habits and manners. He can poke fun at his farmers, but he still reveals a great deal of sympathy for them. He constantly shifts his focus from one character to another, frequently drawing back and spreading his attention over the whole scene, ranging back and forth among the farmers with a cinematographic technique. The over-all effect of the style is to smother the individual people in the vastness of the setting. They are not entirely reduced, because he sweeps in at the last moment for a close-up. In quick succession, for example, the focus changes from Hooven to his daughter, from her to groups of unnamed farmers, from them to Annixter, and so on.

Norris devotes several important paragraphs to a description of the spiritual states of mind of Annixter and Hilma. The girl has been metamorphosed into a woman by love and impending motherhood. As a bearer of life into the world, Hilma takes on universal qualities which Norris describes with epithets very similar to the epithets he uses to describe wheat. She is "serene, entering into her divine right," like a queen. Love gives her a radiance and beauty that is related in some way to mystical universal forces. The force of love has brought Annixter to the understanding of life he described to Presley in the previous chapter, a sense of social responsibility and care for others. The "hardness and inhumanity" in the man has become a kind of vast and humble thankfulness and joy. He is becoming "tolerant and generous, kind and forgiving." The threat of the railroad to take over his home will not yet allow him to assume totally his new character. As soon as he removes the menace, he will broaden into the new man.

Violence has a part in this scene because violence is part of the scheme of nature, part of human nature, and historically part of frontier life. Balance in nature calls for animals to prey on others. Human beings are no exception to the laws of nature. Although the reader may feel a certain horror at the carnage involved in trapping hundreds of rabbits and slaughtering them for food, it is only an emotional aversion. The intellect can easily see the necessity to keep down the number of rabbits in the valley and also the necessity for human nourishment. It is in the scheme of nature that the rabbits die and men feast on them and be jovial.

The event is ironic. It is clearly meant to draw a parallel between the railroad and the farmers. The farmers are as powerless in the grip of the railroad as the rabbits in the trap of the farmers. As **irony** the scene has a certain impact. The parallel is facile and not altogether meaningful, however, since the railroad represents a human organization preying cannibalistically on other humans. There is none of this feeling of cannibalism in the farmers' slaughter of the rabbits.

During the conviviality word comes that the Quien Sabe Ranch has been taken over by the railroad men. The farmers are gathered together in one spot as if an army called together to do battle, but they will not march. Norris prepares the reader in the previous chapter for the failure of the League, when he shows how rumors of unsavory practices are weakening its solidarity. The reasons the farmers present are merely rationalizations for the real reason. For example, they say they cannot go because they are unarmed. That is beside the point, because their enemy is only a dozen men. The actual reason they will not march is because, as a leader, Magnus has failed to inspire them to take action when the time comes for it. Magnus fails them because he fails himself and no longer projects his moral convictions as a bearing of authority.

None of the farmers have stomachs for bloodshed, least of all Annixter, who was truly living according to his philosophy. When the two groups stood face to face, the farmers wanted only to fight with words. Hooven is slightly trigger happy, as his eagerness to shoot rabbits indicates. He fires the first shot, misinterpreting the freak accident that sent farmer Garnett to the ground. No one had time to realize exactly what happened. Given the right circumstances, a chance encounter, and the worst will happen. The consequences of human conduct depend so much on chance that intentions can scarcely be counted. Before anyone can stop the fight, the road is strewn with bodies.

THE OCTOPUS

TEXTUAL ANALYSIS

BOOK II: CHAPTER SEVEN

Wives and families rush to Hooven's house and burst in on the horrible scene of death. Broderson and Harran cling to life for a while, then expire. Osterman hangs on. In a spasm of anger and frustration, Presley declares himself an anarchist like Caraher. While the shattered families are lost in grief, Presley takes up his pen and writes out his anger in a journal. On the following day, the League calls an enormous meeting in Bonneville. Magnus' leadership is severely criticized and the crowd is inflamed by news of Osterman's death that morning. Presley leaps to the stage and delivers a rhetorical address on the idea of freedom, realizing as he speaks that the farmers do not sympathize with his literary approach. Railroad men who have infiltrated the crowd spread extra editions of Genslinger's paper, which carries the bribery story, through the auditorium when Magnus attempts to address the crowd. Chaos reigns. The farmers press Magnus about the bribery scheme and he is forced to admit his part in it.

COMMENT

Good men dead and good women left without husbands and sons is the result of trying to thwart the power of the railroad. Death may have been avoided, perhaps here, perhaps there, but the end result of two opposed forces is the destruction of one of them. Some destruction is subtle and agonizingly slow, like the fall of Magnus, and some is lightning fast, like Dyke's short outlaw career.

Sometimes it comes suddenly, unexpectedly, like the death of Annixter and the other farmers. The horror is as great no matter which form it takes. It is death.

For the women little can be done but to grieve. Enraged, Presley writes in his journal to relieve the oppressive chaos in his mind. His ideas crystallize in the form of rebellion against the social organization which tolerates, practically silently, the destructive encroachment of the large power-hungry company. His rage is specifically toward the railroad, but in a large sense it is turned against all agencies of oppression and power. Similar organizations exist in all states.

In the morning Presley discovers that the railroad, which controls the telegraph, has sealed off all news from the area so they can present their point of view to the world before any other leaks out.

The uproar in the valley centers on the Opera House in Bonneville, where the farmers converge for a meeting. They are in a mood to find a scapegoat to ease their own guilt feelings. Magnus, as leader of the League, receives the blame. With the announcement of Osterman's death, Presley is unable to contain himself. He jumps up and addresses the crowd. He preaches revolution to the polite and impressed - but unsympathetic - ears of the farmers. He speaks well over their heads, throwing out abstract words - Liberty, Revolution - in complex literary allusions. The practical-minded farmers are not deeply moved.

In his anger Presley has violated the lesson Vanamee taught him when he wrote "The Toilers." A work should carry a message, as Presley's speech does, but the message should be simple, straightforward, and sincere. By the time Presley's meaning has been pressed into Biblical **allusions** and rhetorical expressions, he has obscured the message and watered down its apparent sincerity. Presley has separated himself from the farmers as an intellectual and poet. He cannot exercise the force over them that Magnus could at one time command. He is not a political leader.

Compare Presley's speech to the farmers with his diary writings the night before. The flowery language, the elaborate rhetorical devices, the literary **allusions** are all absent from his private writings. The starkness of bone-bare statement marks the diary as the sincere expression of the man. Norris, who is often directly represented by Presley, has very strong ideas about the use of art, and especially the novel, to influence social problems. Naturalism dictates a direct and undecorated style that can be read and appreciated by a person with usual, everyday taste. The truth, in his opinion, is eloquent enough without eloquent language. Presley's failure to capture the imaginations of the farmers is an illustration of that theory of naturalism.

By the time covered by this chapter, Presley has changed from a romantic man without political interests into an anarchist with few literary aspirations. His mind is continually torn with the tension between a romantic view of the West he wants to portray in his **epic**, and a realistic or naturalistic view of the country, which includes events and actualities that do not seem to fit into the romantic view. The awful power struggle with its attendant corruption and death do not seem to Presley to mesh with the glory of the pure earth responding to seed and the attentions of farmers. During this chapter, Presley is so blinded by rage that he can see only the realistic or sordid side of the life and death struggle in the San Joaquin Valley.

The destruction of Magnus Derrick is complete in this chapter. He has lost his two sons, his self-respect, his ability to command the fidelity of the farmers, and will soon lose his land and home. His punishment is far out of proportion to his crime. That is the way of power. Dyke was punished without having committed any crime. The most curious thing about Magnus's failure is that he failed both earlier as a politician and later as leader of the League because he was too good, too well meaning, and too honest to carry out an effective campaign against his opponents. Even the crime of bribery, to which he stooped, although he could scarcely bear the consequences, was an act without criminal motivation. Magnus is a tragic figure, a man of uncommon contributions to the community, who is destroyed without cause.

The implication of Presley's sudden adoption of anarchy along with Caraher, the visit to his saloon, and his determined ride into Bonneville must be that Presley is going to act out the consequences of his newly taken political belief. He tosses the bomb into Behrman's home. The act is extraordinary for Presley, whom the reader knows to be a dreamer, an observer, and a poet rather than a man of action. His slow involvement in the affairs of the Valley, and his consequent loss of detachment show how a man of extraordinary sensibilities is practically forced to action by the injustice of events. Norris defends involvement of artists in social events in his book of essays, *The Responsibilities of a Novelist*, by saying that the artist, especially the novelist, has a social responsibility in addition to an artistic responsibility.

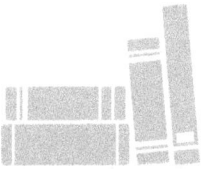

THE OCTOPUS

TEXTUAL ANALYSIS

BOOK II: CHAPTER EIGHT

A month later Presley visits Cedarquist in San Francisco to report the complete defeat of the farmers by the railroad, and to get passage away from California on one of Cedarquist's ships. In his despair as a failure, he wants to find the surviving women of the Hooven family in order to help them before he leaves. Compulsively, he drops in on Shelgrim, the head of the P. and S. W., to see the great enemy first hand, and is shocked at the man's words during the interview. Presley finds Minna Hooven by chance, only to learn to his horror that she has become a prostitute. Oppressed by the sense of failure, Presley dines with the Cedarquists and the Gerards, the family of a vice president of the P. and S. W. The remainder of the chapter chronicles the death of Mrs. Hooven, Minna's mother, by starvation while trying to care for Hilda, ironically inserted in **episodes** in the story of Presley's overly refined dinner with the frivolous upper-class railroad executive.

| COMMENT

Norris has continually presented the point of view of the farmers, leading the reader to identify with them just as Presley does. In his interview with Shelgrim, one of the most important scenes in the novel, Presley is exposed to the railroad's point of view as expressed by a man of great culture and extraordinary understanding. Previously Presley has been exposed only to petty functionaries who could not express the essence of the power they served.

Shelgrim tells Presley that the railroad is a force much like the force of nature as represented by wheat. The railroad came into being by the law of supply and demand. As long as the earth can bring up wheat, it will. As long as the wheat exists, the means of transporting it from the field to the mouths of hungry people will also exist. Shelgrim denies that he has control over the railroad. He is not the company. It would go on without him. It is a living organization dependent on no single man, in the control of no individual. It exists because California and the world needs it. Nothing can stop its progress or its rise to power. Its power is in direct ratio to the need for it to exist.

There is a significant difference between the force incorporated by the wheat and the process of fecundation of the earth that goes into producing it, and the force of the railroad that was born out of the heads of human beings and exists as a parasite living off the distribution of wheat. The railroad is a human-born monster, following the laws of human psychology, especially the basic law of greed for profit. While the wheat is serene, the railroad is opportunistic and avaricious. While nature brings forth wheat and spreads it prodigally over the face of the earth, the railroad is niggardly and self-protective, wasting no energy or wealth on unprofitable, unpragmatic endeavors. Unattended by men, the wheat may rot on the stalks. The railroad never takes such a risk.

The railroad is not outside the laws of nature. The human being, whose avaricious temperament the railroad follows and fosters is avaricious according to the law of nature. The naturalist is careful to point out that human beings have evil in them in some degree. In Chapter One, Magnus Derrick, the man of rigid morality, expressed his desire to get rich at the cost of the railroad. Even in a man of such a natural urge toward good as Magnus, the element of evil lurks somewhere below the surface. Dyke, who was a simple, hard-working, and kind man, of great love and affability, reverted to the conduct of a vicious beast under the suitable circumstances. It is that evil portion of men that the railroad most represents and most inspires in those who adhere to it. However, at the same time the railroad is transporting life nourishment in the form of grain to hungry people all over the country. Thus, not even the railroad is totally evil. In naturalism, nothing is absolutely good or bad, since the literary philosophy is based on a judgment of life far too complex for such a single assumption.

The naturalist's point of view does not assign to nature any morality or tendency toward either good or evil. Nature is indifferent. It carries on in an unchanged, unchanging fashion, generation after generation, without foresight or hindsight, Nature is indifferent, as Presley realizes with a shock just after his interview with Shelgrim. Nature has no vested interests in life on earth. Men are consequently free to act as they will without fearing opposition from nature. Such a judgment of the universe precludes all moral absolutes. It does not preclude God, but makes Him rather beside the point. He, as a part of nature and the creator of nature, has no immediate influence for either good or evil. The moral codes attributed to God must, under this system, be judged by human standards rather than divine standards. Those moral codes are creations of the human spirit rather than the divine. They are, of course, far superior to moral chaos. The Christian character in the novel, Father Sarria, is not an evil character, nor is he an especially good character from the point of view of his influence. He is a zero, a nothing.

After Presley's interview with Shelgrim, the reader can no longer identify totally with the farmers, nor can he devote his total sympathy to them, despite the horror of their destruction. That horror is in the scheme of development given by the law of supply and demand as it existed in the social and political circumstances of the San Joaquin Valley during the historical period covered in the novel. The reader's point of view has been wrenched from the purely local to the over-all. He can now see both sides of the conflict.

More horrors are to follow in the story of Minna Hooven's decline to prostitution under the pressure of the indifferent city. In her wanderings about, trying to find a way to support herself, Minna receives the help of a few people, but it is too little and too late. She is forced into the trap of prostitution to save herself from starvation. The laws of supply and demand, opportunity, chance, and colossal indifference are at work in the story of Minna's fall. She is like the silver ball turning at random on the roulette wheel of chance. The ball falls into a convenient slot.

Minna has been suddenly deprived of her family, her income, her security, and all familiar surroundings. She acts in the only way that seems to be open to her. Norris wishes no moral judgment to be made of her. The judgment must be made of the society which has set her loose without resources and at the same time fostered and supported the trap into which she falls. She is innocent. Norris has weakened his point slightly, presumably in order to achieve credibility, because he suggests in an earlier chapter that Minna could easily fall into a life of easy virtue. During the jackrabbit hunt, Presley observes that she could fall easily, if put under pressure, in the city. Thus, Norris himself equivocates in the fact of the meaning of the total indifference of nature. Minna is not, however, a heroine. She does not possess uncommon strength. She is an average woman, of average resistance to destruction. The trap is far stronger than she is.

The melodramatic last half of this chapter ironically juxtaposes the agonized death by starvation of Mrs. Hooven beside the portrayal of an overly refined and too comfortable family at dinner. Mr. Gerard has benefitted enormously by aligning himself with the avarice and social indifference of the railroad. Mrs. Hooven has lost everything because her husband opposed it. Perhaps Norris rides the **irony** too heavily by his technique of entwining the two stories together, but the melodramatic effect is moving. Mrs. Hooven is a heroic character. She possesses, unlike her eldest daughter, uncommon strength and determination, making her death the more moving when it occurs. Her strength, it must be remarked, comes from her devotion to Hilda. It comes from love.

The **irony** has two edges. Not only does the irony arise from the juxtaposition of the two scenes, but also from the reader's knowledge that Presley is in San Francisco specifically to aid her. Had either one the knowledge of the location of the other, her death would not occur. The point: chance and indifference.

THE OCTOPUS

TEXTUAL ANALYSIS

BOOK II: CHAPTER NINE

....

Behrman, the new owner of the Los Muertos Ranch, has a moment of hollow glory when he joins his workmen on the field combine. He has sold a load of grain to the Famine Committee and contracted Cedarquist's ship, the Swanhilda, to transport it. Presley, who will sail on the Swanhilda, returns to the Valley to say goodbye to his friends, learning that Dyke is sentenced to life imprisonment, the remaining Derricks are leaving, although Magnus is a senile old man. Having changed his political opinion, Presley avoids Caraher. As he looks out over the land before leaving, Presley comprehends what his experience in the Valley means to him. Vanamee appears and contributes to Presley's insight. Meanwhile, in San Francisco, while checking on the progress of his cargo, Behrman is accidentally drowned and suffocated in the flow of wheat.

COMMENT

The railroad men are triumphant in the Valley, having taken over the land just in time to profit from the bonanza wheat crop planted by the dispossessed farmers. Behrman takes his place on the field combine for a few minutes. He is motivated by a combination of greed and exultation. The wheat flowing into the sacks means profit to him, pure profit. He is not aware of the glory of the enormous acreage rendering its fertility in tons of wheat, except as wealth, and he is a pitiful and profane figure with his puny greed in the shadow of the enormous creativity of nature, over which he feels power without having the slightest.

Presley returns to take his departure from his few remaining friends in the Valley. Dyke has been committed to prison for life. His mother and daughter are lost souls who scarcely have reason to continue living without him, especially his mother. Magnus and his wife are going away, although Magnus scarcely has awareness any longer. Behrman offers him a job with the railroad, and Magnus accepts. He is defeated. Hilma Annixter has become profoundly deep and mature, but she is lost and without direction or goals without her husband. Adversity has opened her soul to a kind of inarticulate wisdom to which Presley responds very strongly. He loves her.

As Presley looks out over the endless San Joaquin Valley, brown and dried in the sun, resting before pushing up another crop, he comes to understand that the universe is guided by enormous forces, which are the same on all generations throughout all time. The force of creation brings all things into the world. The force of death removes all things from the world to make room for the new generation. Life and death cease to exist in the face of the enormous forces of creation and destruction, because creation and destruction are the unchanging absolutes of the universe. Creation replaces destruction, and destruction makes way for creation. An individual, a temporary fragment of the great cyclic process, loses all importance by his sheer irrelevance to the great universal forces. Norris suggests that the individual human being is only one of the many means through which the universal forces express themselves. The individual is meaningless; the force is everything.

Vanamee extends Presley's understanding of his insight. The mystic sees only the force of creation in the universe. Creation is life. Death is only the absence of creation, and there is never the true absence of creation. It goes on all the time on all sides. Death has no existence of its own. Life is like the burgeoning of the wheat. Death is like the temporary absence of the wheat. Vanamee speaks as if life is a vast pool of absolute size, and each being shares a portion of it for a space of time and then relinquishes that portion to its source for another individual to use for a span of time. The life never disappears. Only the being which manifests the life passes away.

Of course, Vanamee has found love again with Angele, the daughter of his dead lover. For him she is the same woman, the life mysteriously transferred from the one to the other.

Before he leaves, Vanamee tells Presley, "Evil is short-lived. Never judge the whole round of life by the mere segment you can see. The whole is, in the end, perfect." Such a statement must be understood as the voice of Norris speaking through the mystic. The statement expresses profound optimism and seems to contradict the previous contention that the universe is indifferent, like a huge machine. The laws of the universe are perfect, Norris implies. Suffering and death, deprivation and pain, belong to the lot of mankind. The end result is always progress for the whole of mankind.

It is difficult to reconcile that statement to the events of the novel. Many critics decline to acknowledge that the book supports that concept of the universe. The activities of men, their failures and successes, cannot have importance. Until this chapter, Norris appeared to be persuading the reader to care very much about the failure of Magnus, Minna, Annixter, Dyke, and the other characters. He seemed to want the reader to be outraged at the injustice of the railroad. Suddenly he tells the reader that those events have no importance. On the other hand, as Shelgrim first points out and Vanamee later supports, the railroad is ultimately a force of good. It is a force of good, of course, in its over-all duty as distributor of nourishment. The question Norris leaves unresolved concerns the methods, motivation, and influence applied by the P. and S. W. on the men affiliated with it. Shelgrim has a sort of wisdom, but Behrman and Gerard are despicable characters, as presented by Norris. The over-all influence of the railroad in the San Joaquin Valley is corruptive and destructive. Norris would appear to conclude that the end justifies the means. He does not resolve for the reader the immediate question of how men should conduct themselves in the context of an optimistic universe moving always toward good. Many readers will probably feel that he robs men of their ability to commit a significant action.

The element of chance returns once again as if to support Presley's conclusion that the movement of the universe is toward good. Ironically, Behrman trips and falls into the hold of the Swanhilda and is drowned in his own wheat. Thus, a character who inhibits the progress of the universe toward good is eliminated without revenge by the universe itself. Critics have pointed out that Behrman is not an importantly evil character, since he was only a front man for the railroad power. His death is not so significant a loss to the railroad as to be considered a reduction of their evilness. Those critics suggest that Shelgrim or Gerard should have been accidentally killed. At least, they are men in responsible positions in the company, men who could perhaps have altered the course of events if they had wanted. In any case, it seems clear that Norris wanted to suggest that Behrman's death carried the universe in some way toward good. No one is responsible for Behrman's death, not even he himself. It merely happens, an accident. The force of creation, wheat, destroys the force of destruction, Behrman.

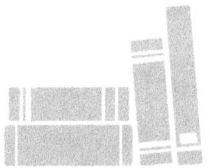

THE OCTOPUS

TEXTUAL ANALYSIS

BOOK II: CHAPTER TEN

Presley speaks to Cedarquist before he boards the Swanhilda for a passage to India. The sale of one of Cedarquist's unsuccessful businesses, the foundry, provides enough money for the creation of another, the shipping company. Presley stands on the deck of the departing ship while the events of his stay in California run through his mind again. He concludes that the good has prevailed despite the suffering, the corruption, and the death.

COMMENT

The Swanhilda is loaded with wheat for the starving masses in the Orient. Cedarquist has acquired enough money through the sale of his defunct foundry to provide for the building of another ship also to carry wheat to India. Lives in India will be saved, justifying the loss of life and the destruction of human beings in California. The over-all view, Norris implies, is progress.

Men are unimportant. The death of Annixter is justified by the saving of lives in India. A life passes, but life itself remains. Life is symbolized by the wheat, "the mighty world force ... indifferent to the human swarm ... falseness dies; injustice and oppression in the end of everything fade and vanish away. Greed, cruelty, selfishness, and inhumanity are short-lived ... The larger view always and through all shams, all wickedness, discovers the truth that will, in the end, prevail, and all things surely, inevitably, resistlessly work together for good." Thus, Norris restates his conclusion. It is no clearer in meaning here than it was in the previous chapter when he introduced it. The truth of the idea is beside the point for the purpose of this study guide. The question to be considered by the student of literature is whether the novel supports its conclusion or whether the conclusion is attached without organic connection. Critics by no means agree on the issue, leaving the reader with the responsibility of formulating his own opinion.

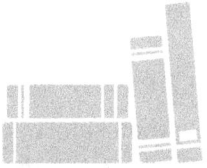

THE OCTOPUS

CHARACTER ANALYSES

PRESLEY

Many events in the novel are reported through Presley's eyes and many of the reader's reactions, opinions and loyalties are determined by his. He is not, however, the hero or **protagonist** of the book in a conventional sense, because he is usually little more than an observer. Often he presents the author's point of view, introducing concepts into the novel, as opposed to other characters who usually illustrate concepts dramatically. Presley is responsible for very little dramatic action.

In the beginning, Presley is a dreamy, sensitive, observant but romantic young man, with no attachment to the San Joaquin Valley or to the political and social events which occur there, except for a vague desire to write an **epic** about the place. He is a poet, cultivated in an eastern university, with a feeling for the grandeur of the wide-open spaces and a desire to write a large work that comprehends that grandeur of nature.

As the farmers become more enmeshed in their fight against the railroad, Presley becomes himself involved out of a sense of loyalty to his friends and out of a distaste for injustice. The farmers accept him into their most secret meetings, but he contributes nothing to the fight until after the farmers have been slain by the railroad men. Then he temporarily adopts the political position of Caraher, an anarchist, and throws a bomb into Behrman's dining room. He also seizes the stage during the League meeting after the gunfight to exhort the farmers to revolution, without impressing them very much.

The only significant action by Presley prior to the skirmish is to author the poem, "The Toilers." The destruction of Dyke provoked the young poet to write the poem. After the skirmish, he is possessed by a sense of failure that drives him to want to help the farmers on the one hand and to want to escape from California on the other. Soon after his speech for revolution, he changes his political opinion to become essentially apolitical, much as he is at the opening of the novel. Within the month, he arranges for passage to India on one of Cedarquist's ships. Before he leaves the state, however, he wants to succeed in some minor way, and attempts to find Hooven's destitute family in San Francisco. He does not succeed in finding them before their separate downfall.

It is Presley's intelligence, aided by Vanamee, which attempts to summarize the action of the book and attribute meaning to the events that transpire. The force of nature embodied in the wheat is either presented directly, by Norris, or indirectly, through Presley's understanding. The ultimate insight is presented through his mind as he looks over the valley on his last visit. Vanamee of course adds to the insight, but it is Presley who is intended by the author to convince the reader of its validity.

In the end, Presley retreats without having written his **epic** and without having contributed substantially to the fight against the railroad.

MAGNUS DERRICK

The railroad represents the "new" politics of power and corruption. Magnus, past politician and miner, and of rigid moral conviction, represents the "old" politics. He is an imposing man with a great gift for leadership, who nevertheless is unable effectively to lead men because his moral rigidity prohibits him from competing against the "new" politics.

He is chosen by the farmers to head their League and is consequently forced to accept the conditions of the fight, including bribery. The need to compromise his moral convictions eats into his self-confidence and self-respect, weakening his ability as a natural leader. Consequently, he is a rather poor leader of the League. His son, Lyman, is corrupted by the P. and S. W., a great blow to the stately old man. His other son, Harran, is killed in the skirmish. Finally the newspaper reveals his part in the bribery, and the old man is totally defeated, becoming senile and incompetent.

One of the main threads in the novel is the decline of Magnus under the corruptive force of the railroad. Magnus is not equipped to resist such a program of harassment, bribery, corruption, power, and extortion as the railroad brings to bear on him. Norris means to show the destruction of a good man, although he suggests on one occasion that Magnus has a greed for money. In Magnus, the desire for wealth is severely controlled by a fundamental moral repugnance to injustice and exploitation.

In the end, the old man is a mere shell of his former self, reduced to working for his former enemies.

LYMAN DERRICK

This son of Magnus Derrick is an opportunist who has adopted the modern ways of achieving his aspirations. He is contrasted with his father, since both have political aspirations. Magnus has failed. Lyman cooperates with the railroad in the destruction of his father in order to enlist the enormous political power of the railroad on his behalf. The implication is that he will succeed in getting the governorship by the "new" politics that his father was unable to accept.

HARRAN DERRICK

This son of Magnus is a weak reflection of his father, but he at least remains loyal to the family. He is a competent rancher and a responsible citizen who gives his life for the cause of the League. He is not an especially talented man. In his more easy acceptance of the League's methods, he represents a more modern man than his father, but not so modern as his brother Lyman.

MRS. DERRICK

Magnus's wife is a rather weak and self-indulgent woman who swings along with the popular view in artistic and cultural matters, except for her firm opposition to Magnus's joining the League. She is significantly at fault in that she does not seem ever to realize the magnitude of the trap her husband is caught in. She remains loyal to the end, intending to return to her job as a teacher after her husband and sons have been destroyed.

ANNIXTER

As with Magnus, the story of Annixter is one of the main threads in the novel. As first introduced to the reader in a conversation with Presley, Annixter is a cranky, irritable, self-centered misfit who can farm well, but whose life is r succession of frustrations. He has a strong aversion to women, fearing that they will trap him and bind his life. He has no insight into himself, continually misinterpreting his own motives.

When he notices Hilma Tree, one of his dairymaids, he is unable to determine what relationship he would like with her. He blunders and alienates her. Slowly he wins back her goodwill and, eventually, a declaration of love. His mind cannot conceive of marriage and he blunders again by asking her to be his mistress. When she leaves him, he is forced to come to an understanding with himself about what she means to him. Suddenly his whole character changes. He seeks out Hilma in San Francisco and marries her. As a result of love he loses his selfishness and defensiveness. He comes to understand that love is the only important thing in life, and love leads to social awareness and responsibility. He wants to help others, to think for the ignorant, and to support the poor. The revolution in Annixter's character is dramatic and complete, perhaps too dramatic and too complete, suggest some critics. Nevertheless, a major thematic thread in the novel is expressed by the change in Annixter's character. The entry of love into a man's life may change his character very much for the better. Love itself fosters further love in a general way toward others. Annixter's love is a motivation and a guide the way a strict moral code is a motivation and guide for Magnus, who is a rather austere and loveless man. Beside the "old" politics of service and the "new" politics of power, Norris juxtaposes this third nonpolitical way of life, the way of love and paternalism as expressed by Annixter to Presley on the morning that Dyke arrives in his flight from the posse.

HILMA (TREE) ANNIXTER

She is an inactive character in the novel, although she motivates Annixter to his major insight. She is initially portrayed as pure innocence and joy of living. Annixter seems to her brutal until after he realizes that he loves her. With the marriage she becomes matronly. After Annixter's death, Norris suggests in the last meeting between her and Presley, that she arrives at full maturity as a woman of profound understanding of the tragedy of life. In some way she is like the wheat itself. She remains, after all the activity and destruction, unconquered and unbroken, but profoundly changed and deepened by the events. Norris implies that she will resume a new life, perhaps with a new man, but will never totally be free of the imprint of her first husband. The joy of living is no longer present in her life, but a sense of the meaning of living seems to be present in some inarticulate way.

VANAMEE

This mystic, whose story enters episodically into the narrative, helps Presley to his ultimate insight during their last meeting together. Norris calls Vanamee the "born poet" as opposed to Presley the "made poet."

After the death of Angele, his lover, Vanamee becomes a wandering hermit and mystic. His conduct is instinctual and unintellectual, disengaged and uncommitted. No one understands him, but he seems to understand everyone else. He is close to the soil and to the forces of nature, possessing the unusual spiritual gift of psychic communication.

The daughter of his lover comes to him in response to his psychic summons in the Mission yard. She is a replacement for her mother and he transfers his love to her. For him there is no significant difference between mother and daughter. He identifies the change from mother to daughter with the cycle of the seasons, the growth of the wheat and the blooming of the flowers. He passes that idea on to Presley in the form of extreme optimism: from bad comes good, all things tend toward the good, and all things are good if viewed with sufficient perspective.

Vanamee is embittered by the loss of love. He turns his scorn against Father Sarria and mocks the priest's Christian God. With the return of love, he becomes a teleological optimist.

FATHER SARRIA

The Spanish priest has little force in the novel, suggesting that Christianity, which he represents, is of little moral force in the Valley. No other character in the book professes to live by Christian ethics. To Magnus, for example, Christianity is beside the point. His ethics are founded on humanism. Norris belittles the Father by showing him discovered in a lie about the fighting cocks. He is a simple man, unable to defend Christianity under the sting of Vanamee's scorn, but he is a good man who expends much energy helping the less fortunate families in the Valley. His strength and understanding of life are woefully inadequate to engage in a fight of the magnitude of the farmers' resistance to the railroad.

DYKE

After being twice double-crossed by the railroad, Dyke lashes out and is destroyed by it. He is an affable man of great loyalty, both to the railroad when he was an engineer and to his agricultural responsibilities when he is a hops farmer. He would like to be wealthy, but not for wealth itself. He has plans to take care of his mother and to send his daughter to school. Once ruined by the railroad's arbitrary raise in the shipping rate for hops, Dyke becomes a vicious animal. He robs the train for revenge and kills a guard in the process. The railroad runs him down like an animal and the courts imprison him for life. Everybody likes Dyke, including the reader, and his downfall is moving. Norris means to emphasize the viciousness of the railroad power and the total futility of fighting it singlehandedly.

BEHRMAN

The power of the P. and S. W. in the San Joaquin Valley is personified by S. Behrman, a despicable man whom Norris always describes in the most disagreeable manner. He is fat and repulsive to look at. He has no manners and no morals. The power of the company he represents gives him great confidence and an overbearing attitude which he preserves even under great duress. He will not argue or take a stand on an issue, except as ordered by his superiors in San Francisco. In short, he is a monster, motivated by a desire for wealth and power, with no redeeming features at all.

When he tries to be friendly he is monstrously ironic, as when he offers Magnus a job with the railroad after it has taken the man's land, destroyed his sons, and broken his spirit. It is too much to believe that Behrman was moved by pity at that late moment in the story of his crimes. He simply does not understand anything that does not have to do with the acquisition of wealth. Further, the job offer itself is an arrogant display of the power of railroad, with its affluent attitude toward the victim it claimed.

SHELGRIM

As head of the P. and S. W. Shelgrim bears a great deal of responsibility for events in the San Joaquin Valley. He is a giant of a man whose energy is endless. In his interview with Presley he absolves himself from responsibility for the crimes of the railroad by claiming that the railroad represents a force that responds to the law of supply and demand, rather than to the controlling hand of any man. Presley is moved by the man's words. (They are, however, specious platitudes which do not in any way absolve railroad management from responsibility for the company's crimes. In view of the corruption of the legislature, the court, and the press, the techniques of harassment and force, and the relentless determination of the railroad to press its projects to completion without regard for consequences, the men of the railroad must be held responsible.)

CEDARQUIST

Although an industrialist, Cedarquist is not an evil man who aspires to great power and wealth. He has ambitions, to be sure, but he is a humanist who considers the social consequences of his actions. Some of the guilt of the railroad rubs off on him by association, but he is merely negligent rather than vicious. He takes part in the dinner with the Gerards, a vice president of the P. and S. W., and moves in their society without significant protest. His shipping company provides the ship which carries wheat to India for the Famine Relief Committee, but not without a certain eye to profit. Norris presents the man with sufficient fineness of character for the reader to feel that if Cedarquist were in control of the railroad, the company would be much more kindly.

CARAHER

The anarchist has a subtle influence on events in the novel. His position is essentially negative and leads to chaos and destruction, Presley decides after he has thrown the bomb into Behrman's dining room. Norris does not expand on Caraher's political beliefs. The saloon keeper, as an anarchist, must stand against the League as much as against the railroad, since both are organizations of a certain power. That the Pinkerton police accidentally killed his wife during a railroad strike is presented as Caraher's political motivation, which is a form of nihilism. Norris suggests that Caraher influenced Dyke to strike out singlehandedly against the railroad power.

OSTERMAN

This farmer plays an important role in the development of the League. It was his idea initially that the ranchers band together and bribe politicians to represent them on the Railroad Commission. He also takes a lead in the formulation of the League at Annixter's barn dance the night notification arrives of the railroad's intention to sell their land at outrageous prices.

As a man, Osterman is average, without outstanding talent or understanding of the possible consequences of his actions. He is the man who actually arranges for the bribes, and also one of the men who brings great pressure on Magnus Derrick to join the League as its leader. He has ambitions to preserve his land and make a profit, but not overly so. He has no grand plan for wealth and power. Osterman exhibits a flash of heroism, after the skirmish in the irrigation ditch, when he refuses medical treatment until the other wounded are cared for.

BRODERSON

A rancher in the inner circle of the League, Broderson is an old man who does not understand the magnitude of the farmers' struggle with the railroad. He is a follower who has difficulty making up his mind, and quick to change and qualify his opinions. He is honorable and respectably modest, but determined to fight to have his land. As a follower, he contributes little to the League other than his status as a successful rancher and an upstanding citizen of the community.

HOOVEN

The German immigrant is a common farmer whose well-being depends on the course of action taken by Magnus and the other large ranchers. He is a likable character and useful on the farm. As a tenant farmer, he is a straw in the wind of social consequences. Slightly aggressive and hasty, Hooven fires the first shot in the fight at the irrigation ditch.

MINNA AND MRS. HOOVEN

The stories of Minna and Mrs. Hooven are digressions from the main line of the novel, but they express social consequences which Norris wants to stress. Minna becomes a prostitute to avoid starvation after several days of looking for work in San Francisco. She is perhaps a little weak in her resistance to that fate, but she illustrates Norris's thesis well. Her mother, Mrs. Hooven, a much stronger person, although less intelligent, dies of starvation in San Francisco when she runs out of money and is unable to find food or shelter. Those two women are not guilty of moral wrong, Norris implies. The indifferent society which forces them to their downfall is the guilty party.

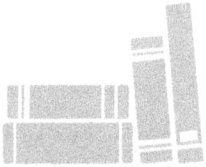

THE OCTOPUS

CRITICAL COMMENTARY

....

Critics have attacked *The Octopus* with a certain vehemence - from the reviewers who found it vulgar when it first came out to the literary historians who now look back at it as too romantic and evasive. The early reviewers now appear ridiculous; of course, they were judging from the point of view of average members of their epoch. The standard of turn-of-the-century reviewers for literature was that a book could be read around the dinner table with all members of the family present.

The most acute critical intelligence of the modern period to discuss Norris is Malcolm Cowley in an essay, "A Natural History of American Naturalism," which appears in *Evolutionary Thoughts in America* (Yale University Press, 1950). Cowley points out that Norris confused physical laws of the universe with social laws. Darwin's law of natural selection can be understood as a social law as well as a physical law. The law of supply and demand, however, cannot be elevated to that level. It is as if the force of the railroad were like the force of gravity. Cowley is unable to accept that supposition. Such a law takes away all sense of human responsibility, reducing man to a mere pawn of universal forces. By taking away man's responsibility, there can be no optimism and no ultimate good that includes man. Without responsibility, man has no capacity to judge good or evil. The book thus contains a fundamental inconsistency.

Cowley also takes Norris to task for his disinterest in style. Style is a means of containing meaning in words. Not to exploit style reduces the ability of the language to convey meaning. Meaning is literature. About style Norris said, "We don't want literature, we want life." The vacillations of Norris's style betray his innate romanticism, a posture which is contradictory to naturalism. The style of romanticism violates the stylistic rule that naturalism must be vigorously objective.

Vernon Parrington balks at the optimistic end of *The Octopus*, remarking that Norris changes his attitude and takes refuge in a "moral attitude." The dramatic action of the novel supports no such moral attitude, observes Parrington, John Chamberlin and Granville Hicks reject the ending as confused, moralistic, and specious for the same reason that Parrington does.

Other critics have argued that Norris was unable to amalgamate the parts of his book into an artistic whole. The original determinism of naturalism turns into tragic action in a vicious society, and then optimistically becomes a good that will triumph. Those three threads cannot exist simultaneously in an artistic whole. Norris does violence to art by leaping from one to the next without transition, as mere acts of faith.

George W. Meyer acknowledges that nature produces wheat, but he does not acknowledge that Norris can generalize that nature is good as a result of having produced the wheat. Nature feeds some and kills others, Meyer observes. Nature is only a fact, not a law.

Many critics find that Shelgrim's defense of the railroad as a force that will grow beyond the control of man is false and specious. He twists words into meaningless statements in order to absolve himself and his organization from responsibility for the company's actions. He is, of course, responsible, maintain the critics, wondering whether Norris himself meant the man's statements seriously.

Granville Hicks and other critics find Norris's handling of characters unsatisfactory. In *The Great Tradition* (The Macmillan Co., 1933), Hicks scoffs at the transformation of Annixter's character by love. There is a contradiction between the tenets of naturalism and such a sudden transformation. In short, Annixter represents Norris's romanticism showing through. One of the most important **themes** in the novel is greatly reduced by Hick's judgment, since the power of love to bring social responsibility is not acceptable in the deterministic framework of naturalism.

Ernest Marchand considers *The Octopus* an unsuccessful naturalistic novel because the moral and philosophical issues are not clear cut. Norris was unable to decide whether he thought good and evil were absolute universal forces or whether they were human concepts. The result of Norris's indecision is a faulty novel, in the estimation of Marchand.

It can be clearly seen that the major issues to be handled by a critic are few but essential. Norris was a romantic who adopted naturalism without being able to maintain the objectivity required by it, and without fully understanding determinism. His romanticism shows through not only in his confusion of **themes** but also in his literary style. The result in *The Octopus* is a novel of very great strengths and very great weaknesses. All of the critics admit that Norris, although faulty, is a major transitional figure between end-of-the-century romanticism and twentieth-century realism.

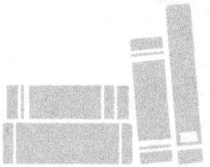

THE OCTOPUS

ESSAY QUESTIONS AND ANSWERS

Question: In what way does Norris oppose the individual to Nature?

Answer: One **theme** of *The Octopus* is the indifference of vast nature, in which the individual is swallowed up as if a mere "mote in the sun." When Presley finishes "The Toilers," he sets out to find Vanamee somewhere in the vast expanse of the valley. When he finds him, the mystic is kneeling beside a fire, illuminated by its small light, while the infinite space of the earth and sky seemed to press around him, almost smashing him to oblivion. A similar effect is intended in the scene where Vanamee is plowing the Quien Sabe Ranch. The man is miniscule on the enormous machine, and yet the machine itself is dwarfed by the vast countryside. The rain that falls during the night Annixter goes to Los Muertos to attend the first ranchers' meeting has a similar intention to dwarf man. Many other scenes carry out that theme.

Question: Does Norris express the idea of fate?

Answer: Although there is no idea of fate as contained in the Greek epics or in some Christian theology, Norris expresses an idea of determinism by forces outside of the control of human beings. The wheat is a force coming directly from the force of nature. The railroad is another force, obeying the law of supply and demand, a law outside the control of man. Norris implies that men have free will to control their actions, but in the overall picture they are being driven by great universal forces that they cannot oppose. Although the forces are universal, they take on different forms at different periods of history. The law of supply and demand, a universal law, produces the railroad during the period and at the location covered in this novel, but Norris mentions that all over the country other organizations, responding to the law of supply and demand, are oppressing the "People." The conclusion of the novel is that all forces tend toward eventual good, a thesis slightly contradictory to the body of the novel. The over-all view of both determinism and teleology (as the concluding idea is normally called) is the reduction of the human being to a position of no importance in the universe and the inflation of the mass of human beings to a position of strong influence as a source of some forces.

Question: Does *The Octopus* suggest solutions to social and economic problems?

Answer: The conclusion of *The Octopus* suggests that social and economic problems, although never completely disappearing as problems, will solve themselves in such a way that the over-all direction is toward progress. Social and economic problems follow social and economic laws, as if those laws were laws of the universe. Many critics disagree that social and economic laws can be elevated to the height of inevitability of natural law. In his handling of Annixter's character, Norris suggests another solution to social and economic laws through love. Annixter, as a result of his love for Hilma, desires to think for the stupid and pay for the poor. Thus, the experience of specific love, his love for his wife and hers for him, gives Annixter a general love for all people and a desire to help them. It is difficult, as some critics have remarked, to believe that Annixter's character can be so profoundly changed by his experience. Norris does, however, advance the theme, and it must be considered as an alternative to the inexorable working out of social and economic problems by impersonal forces.

Question: Why is Vanamee a "born" poet and Presley a "made" poet?

Answer: The reader may infer from Vanamee's character what Norris thinks a poet is. Vanamee is a mystic who attaches himself to no material things, a man whose most powerful emotion is a love which remains faithful for two decades to a woman who no longer lives. He has no apparent drive to acquire wealth and remains separated from all other people and yet understands them. He has enormous sympathy for men and appears to understand the meaning of the universe and to be adjusted to it, except for his powerful drive to find again the woman he loves. The emotion of love and his adjustment to the condition of mankind are the two strongest elements in his personality. He blends into the laws of nature. As a poet, however, Vanamee seems to have no desire to produce literary works or to be known as a literary man. At the same time, although not a mystic, Presley shares some of the mystic's qualities. He has great sympathy for human beings, although less than Vanamee. In Chapter Two, Norris notes that Presley would be offended by the manners of the plow drivers at dinner. He has a desire to understand what happens in the universe and why men are as they are. Presley takes sides with the farmers against the railroad, an attitude Vanamee cannot assume. The mystic is somehow apart from and above all events, as if standing on a mountain and viewing the works of mankind far below him. Presley has trouble understanding where his great epic lies in the mass of events in the Valley, whereas Vanamee seems to know exactly how the struggle evokes the general condition of mankind along with the particular conditions of the specific struggle. Presley has attended a university and studied the works of great writers, and his judgments of life are somehow influenced by them, as is shown by his constant reference to Homer. Vanamee's understanding and judgments come only from experience and self-study, carried out, presumably, during his many years of solitude.

Question: What does Vanamee mean when he says: "Evil is short-lived. Never judge of the whole round of life by the mere segment you can see. The whole is, in the end, perfect."

Answer: Vanamee is closer to love and nature than to the railroad and other corruptive forces in the world. Although he is acutely aware of the power of evil for the destruction of the love object, he has faith that love itself cannot be destroyed. Love is a more potent emotion than desire for wealth. The struggles of mankind, birth and death, are all proper to the life of man. Vanamee has gained all of his understanding through direct contemplation of experience. His experience is the rebirth of his lover after her evil destruction. As a "born" poet and a mystic in tune with the spiritual vibrations of the universe, Vanamee's experience is supposed to be typical, a paradigm of mankind's experience. Just as the wheat returns season after season, irrepressibly, love also returns. The other assumption lying behind Vanamee's statement is that there is a goal toward which all things move. The goal is perfect, he says. The implication is that the universe is going through some sort of evolutionary process, working toward perfection. Such a conclusion is an article of faith, impossible to prove. The whole point of view expressed by Vanemee is consequently a matter of faith. The great power and attraction of this optimistic point of view is that it can give comfort to the distraught man whose life is degenerating before his eyes.

BIBLIOGRAPHY

WORKS BY FRANK NORRIS

Moran of the Lady Letty: A Story of Adventure Off the California Coast. New York: Doubleday & McClure Co., 1898.

McTeague: A Story of San Francisco. New York: Grosset & Dunlap, n.d.

Blix. New York: Doubleday & McClure Co., 1899.

A Man's Woman. New York: Doubleday & McClure Co., 1900.

The Octopus: A Story of California. New York: Doubleday, Page & Co., 1901.

The Pit: A Story of Chicago. New York: Doubleday, Page & Co., 1903.

A Deal in Wheat, and Other Stories of the New and Old West. New York: Doubleday, Page & Co., 1903.

The Responsibilities of the Novelist, and Other Literary Essays. New York: Doubleday, Page & Co., 1903.

The Joyous Miracle. New York: Doubleday, Page & Co., 1906.

Vandover and the Brute. New York: Doubleday, Page & Co., 1914.

The Third Circle. New York: Dodd, Mead & Co., 1922.

Complete Works. New York: Doubleday, *Doran & Co., 1928 (10 vols.).*

WORKS ABOUT FRANK NORRIS

Books

Ahnebrink, Lars. *The Beginnings of Naturalism in American Fiction.* New York: Russell & Russell, 1961.

———. *The Influence of Emile Zola on Frank Norris.* Cambridge: Harvard University Press, 1947.

Cargill, Oscar. *Intellectual America.* New York: The Macmillan Company, 1941.

French, Warren. *Frank Norris.* New York: Twayne Pub., 1962.

Hicks, Granville. *The Great Tradition.* New York: The Macmillan Company, 1933.

The Letters of Frank Norris, ed. Franklin Walker. San Francisco, 1956.

Marchand, Ernest. *Frank Norris: A Study.* Stanford: Stanford University Press, 1942.

Parrington, Vernon L. *The Beginnings of Critical **Realism** in America*, 1860–1920 (Vol. III of Main Currents in American Thought). New York: Harcourt, Brace and Co., 1930.

Walker, Franklin. *Frank Norris: A Biography*. Garden City: Doubleday, Doran and Co., Inc., 1932.

ARTICLES

Meyer, George W. "A New Interpretation of *The Octopus*," *College English*, IV (March, 1943), 351–359.

Pfizer, Donald. "Another Look at *The Octopus*," *Nineteenth-Century Fiction*, X (December, 1955), 217–224.

Reninger, H. Willard. "Norris Explains *The Octopus*: A Correlation of His Theory and Practice," *American Literature*, VII (May, 1940), 218–227.

www.ingramcontent.com/pod-product-compliance
Lightning Source LLC
LaVergne TN
LVHW011727060526
838200LV00051B/3061